CANADIAN

PRIVATE SECURITY HANDBOOK

A PRACTICAL REFERENCE FOR CANADIAN SECURITY PROFESSIONALS

THIS BOOK BELONGS TO:

SIGNATURE:

Table of Contents

Legal Disclaimer

This book provides general information for educational purposes only. It is not legal advice and does not replace legal counsel, your employer's policies, or the specific licensing requirements of your province or territory.

Laws, regulations, and licensing requirements referenced in this book change over time and vary by jurisdiction. Confirm current requirements directly with your provincial or territorial regulator before relying on any information in this book.

The author and publisher make no warranty, express or implied, regarding the accuracy or completeness of this information, and accept no liability for any loss or damage arising from its use. Always follow your employer's specific procedures and consult a lawyer for guidance on any legal matter.

About the Author

Ryan Heath spent over 20 years working in and leading security operations in Alberta, specializing in nightclub, event, and high rise building security. Ryan has founded and operated several of his own private security agencies. He built and ran these agencies from the ground up, providing mobile patrol units, alarm response, stationary security personnel, investigations, and security consulting for clients across the region.

Ryan has managed building security operations for commercial properties and government offices. He has conducted physical site security surveys and led hazard assessments and crime prevention consulting for clients across multiple industries. He designed and delivered a training program for nightclub security personnel, and trained commercial non-security staff in emergency response procedures. As a certified parking bylaw officer, he enforced City of Red Deer parking bylaws and handled bylaw compliance duties alongside his core security work.

Over two decades, Ryan built his knowledge through direct field experience: patrol operations, incident response, client consulting, staff training, and agency ownership. He has trained dozens of security personnel and advised organizations on physical security planning and risk reduction.

Ryan wrote the Canadian Security Guard Handbook to put that field knowledge into the hands of new and working guards. The book draws on two decades of firsthand experience running security operations across Alberta. It gives readers the practical knowledge that usually takes years on the job to learn: how to write a report that holds up, how to handle a complicated scene, how licensing and provincial regulations actually work, and how to build a career in the industry.

Ryan lives in Red Deer, Alberta, where he continues to work in high level property management services alongside his writing.

Foreword

This book exists because most guards learn the real job after they are already on shift, not before. Basic license training covers the legal minimum. It does not cover how to talk someone down from a bad night, how to write a report that holds up months later, or how to build the kind of reputation that gets you promoted.

This handbook fills that gap. It is written for the guard standing at a desk at 2 a.m., the new hire walking into their first shift, and the supervisor training someone who has never worn the uniform before.

How to Use This Book

Read Sections 1 through 4 before you apply for your license. They will help you decide if this career fits you, and they will prepare you for the application and hiring process.

Keep Sections 5 through 13 close once you are working. These cover the practical skills you will use on shift: communication, report writing, emergency response, and professional conduct. Come back to them as situations arise that you want a refresher on..

Treat Sections 14 and 15 as reference material for your ongoing career. Legal knowledge and career growth are not one time lessons. Revisit them as your role changes and your experience grows.

The appendices are built for quick reference. Keep the phonetic alphabet chart and the sample report templates where you can find them fast, whether that means a printed copy in your vehicle or duty bag or a saved file on your phone.

Who This Book Is For

This handbook is written for:

- New applicants deciding whether a security career is right for them.
- Newly licensed guards preparing for their first posting.
- Experienced guards looking to sharpen specific skills or move toward a supervisor role.
- Trainers and supervisors who want a consistent reference to give to new hires.

This is not a substitute for your provincial licensing training, your employer's site specific procedures, or legal advice for a specific situation. It is the practical companion to all three, built from the questions new guards ask most and the mistakes that have cost them the most. This guide is what I wish I had been given all those years ago when I started my security career.

First shift?

May 12

SECTION 01

IS SECURITY WORK RIGHT FOR YOU

- Observe
- Communicate
- Document

Stay alert.

AM I A GOOD FIT?

- ☐ Good communicator
- ☐ Calm under pressure
- ☐ Observant
- ☐ Reliable
- ☐ Good judgment

Professionalism matters.

Every incident is a story.

Could I do this every day?

Canada

Section 1: Is Security Work Right for You

Security work looks simple from the outside. You stand at a desk. You walk around a building. You watch a screen. The reality is different. This job tests your patience, your judgment, and your ability to stay calm when things go wrong. Before you apply for a license or send out a resume, you need an honest picture of what the work demands.

What the Job Actually Involves Day to Day

Most shifts are quiet. You check doors. You log visitors. You write patrol notes. You answer questions from tenants, staff, or customers. Nothing happens for hours at a time.

Then something happens fast: a fight breaks out, fire alarm triggers, person refuses to leave... You need to switch from routine to response in seconds.

Your daily tasks depend on your posting:

- Static guards monitor one location and control access.
- Mobile patrol guards drive between sites and check multiple sites per shift.
- Concierge guards greet visitors and manage building access in residential or office towers.
- Loss prevention officers watch for theft in retail stores, often in plain clothes.
- Event security guards manage crowds, check tickets, and handle disputes at concerts, sports games, or festivals.

Each posting has a different rhythm. Static work rewards patience. Mobile work rewards independence. Retail work rewards observation skills. Know which style fits you before you commit to a role.

Physical and Mental Demands

You spend long hours on your feet. Many shifts run 8 to 12 hours. Some guards walk 10,000 steps or more per shift on patrol. Cold warehouses, hot, dusty equipment yards, and outdoor lots in winter are common environments. Your body needs to handle physical strain and weather extremes.

The mental side is harder to prepare for. You deal with angry people, you deal with people in crisis, you make decisions with incomplete information, often alone. Boredom during slow shifts can be as draining as stress during busy ones.

Ask yourself these questions:

- Can you stay alert during six hours of silence, then react instantly if needed?
- Can you stay calm when someone yells at you or calls you names and degrades you?
- Can you make a decision without a supervisor standing next to you?
- Can you write a clear report at 3 a.m. after a stressful incident?

If you answered yes to all four, you have the right mindset for this work.

Shift Work and Lifestyle Impact

Security runs 24 hours a day. That means night shifts, weekend shifts, and holiday shifts. New guards often start with the least desirable hours. Overnight shifts pay more in some companies, but they disrupt sleep and social life.

Rotating shifts affect your body clock. Fixed night shifts can affect your relationships and social calendar. Talk to your family before you accept a schedule. Guards who ignore this step often burn out or quit within the first year.

Some guards prefer night work. Fewer people, less noise, and a set routine appeal to certain personalities. Know your own preference before you pick a shift type to aim for.

Pay Expectations Across Provinces

Security pay varies by province, employer, and posting type.

General ranges for entry-level security guards in Canada, as of 2026:

Province

Typical Hourly Range

Ontario

$18 to $23

Alberta

$18 to $24

British Columbia

$18 to $22

Quebec

$16 to $20

Manitoba

$16 to $19

Atlantic provinces

$15 to $18

Specialized roles pay more. Executive protection, armored transport, and industrial site security can exceed $30 per hour. Supervisor and management roles can pay more still.

Check current rates in your area before you accept a job offer. Wages shift with inflation, demand, and provincial minimum wage changes.

Career Paths in Security

Security work is not a dead end. Many guards use the job as a stepping stone.

Common paths include:

- **Supervisor or site manager.** You oversee a team, handle scheduling, and manage client relationships.
- **Investigator.** You handle theft cases, fraud, or workplace investigations.
- **Loss prevention manager.** You run theft prevention programs for retail chains.
- **Executive protection agent.** You protect high profile clients, often with specialized training.
- **Law enforcement or corrections.** Many police services and correctional agencies value security experience on an application.
- **Business owner.** Experienced guards start their own security companies once they understand licensing and contracts.

Your first year in the field teaches you which path fits your strengths. Pay attention to what energizes you and what drains you.

Common Misconceptions About the Job

New applicants often misunderstand what the work involves. Clear these up before you start.

Misconception: Security guards have police powers. You do not. You have citizen's arrest powers, which are narrower and more restrictive than police authority. Section 3 covers this in detail.

Misconception: The job is mostly confrontation. Most shifts involve no conflict at all. Confrontation happens, but it is the exception, not the rule.

Misconception: Anyone can do this job. Licensing requires a clean criminal record, specific training, and often a test. Employers also look for judgment and communication skills, not just a license.

Misconception: The pay is not worth it. Entry pay is modest, but specialized postings and supervisor roles pay well. Guards who invest in training and certifications increase their earning potential quickly.

Misconception: You need a criminal justice degree. Most entry-level jobs require only your provincial license and basic training. A degree helps for advancement, but it is not required to start.

A Final Check Before You Commit

Security work suits people who stay calm under pressure, communicate clearly, and take responsibility seriously. It does not suit people who need constant excitement or who struggle with authority and rules.

Read the rest of this handbook before you apply for your license. If the daily reality described here still appeals to you, you are ready to move to Section 2 and start the licensing process.

Requirements vary.

Check provincial regulator.

Licence ≠ Authority.

SECTION 02

LICENSING AND REGULATIONS BY PROVINCE

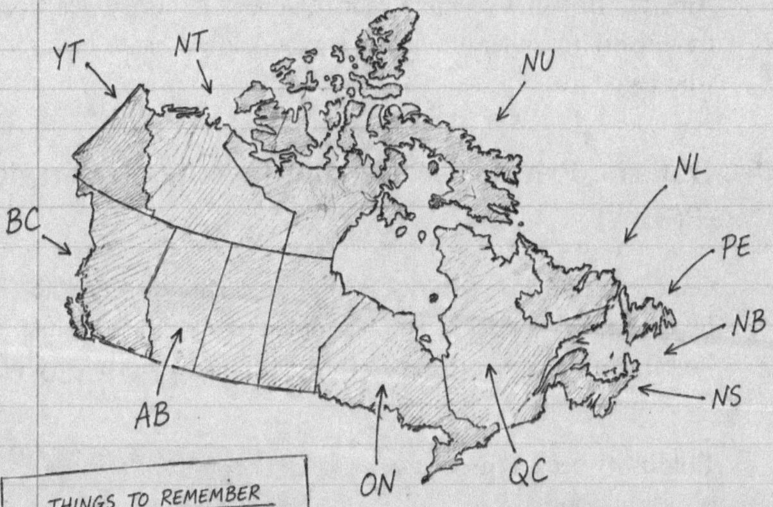

THINGS TO REMEMBER

- [x] Requirements differ.
- [x] Training standards differ.
- [x] Application processes differ.
- [x] Fees differ.
- [x] Renewal periods differ.
- [x] Rules change.

Verify often.

VERIFY CURRENT REQUIREMENTS

Know YOUR jurisdiction.

Section 2: Licensing and Regulations by Province

You cannot work as a security guard in Canada without a license. Every province regulates the industry through its own act and its own licensing body. The rules share a common structure: training, a background check, an application, and a renewal cycle. The details differ enough that you need to check the exact requirements for the province where you plan to work.

This section covers the four largest licensing regimes in detail: Ontario, Alberta, British Columbia, and Quebec. It also gives you the general framework for other provinces, so you know what to look for regardless of where you live.

Ontario: Private Security and Investigative Services Act (PSISA)

Ontario regulates security work through the Private Security and Investigative Services Act, administered by the Private Security and Investigative Services Branch (PSISB) under the Ministry of the Solicitor General.

Eligibility requirements:

- You must be at least 18 years old.
- You must be legally entitled to work in Canada.
- You must not have a conviction for any of the 83 designated offences listed in Ontario Regulation 363/07. These offences bar you from licensing unless you received a pardon.

Training and testing:

- Complete a Ministry approved 40 hour basic training course covering law, use of force, emergency response, and limits of authority.

- Pass the licensing exam, a multiple choice test on the course material.
- Obtain current Standard First Aid and CPR-C certification. Most employers require this even though the PSISA does not always mandate it directly.

Background check:

- Since February 2024, Ontario requires a Criminal Record and Judicial Matters Check (CRJMC) instead of the older Criminal Record Check. A CRJMC is a Level 2 police record check that includes convictions, outstanding charges, and certain judicial orders.
- The CRJMC must come from a police service. Non-police background check providers are not accepted.
- The check must be completed within six months of your application date.

Applying:

- Submit your application online through the Ontario licensing portal once you have your training completion number and CRJMC.
- Licenses are digital only. Ontario no longer issues physical cards. You must carry your digital license and be ready to show it on duty.

Ontario is currently reviewing the PSISA through a 2026 regulatory consultation. Proposed changes include giving the registrar discretion over some disqualifying offences instead of an automatic bar. Check the Ministry website for the current status before you rely on any specific offence list.

Alberta: Security Services and Investigators Act (SSIA)

Alberta regulates security work through the Security Services and Investigators Act, administered by the Security Programs branch of Alberta Justice.

Eligibility requirements:

- You must be at least 18 years old.
- You must meet an English fluency standard equivalent to Canadian Language Benchmark level 5.
- You must pass a criminal record check, including fingerprints in some cases.

Training and testing:

- Complete the Alberta Basic Security Training (ABST) course through an approved provider.
- Pass the provincial exam.
- If you plan to drive a patrol vehicle, you need a valid Class 5 operator's license.

License details:

- The fee is $100.
- Your license is valid for two years.
- Your license is portable. It stays valid if you switch employers or work for more than one employer at once.
- You cannot hold a security worker license and a locksmith or automotive lock bypass license at the same time.
- If you work as an independent contractor offering security services, you need both an guard license and an agency license at the same time.

Alberta issues licenses through the Registrar of Security Services. Contact information: Security Programs, Alberta Justice, P.O. Box 1023 Station Main, Edmonton, Alberta T5J 2M1. Phone 1-877-462-0791.

British Columbia: Security Services Act

British Columbia regulates security work through the Security Services Act, administered by the Security Programs Division of the Ministry of Public Safety and Solicitor General.

Eligibility requirements:

- You must be at least 19 years old for most security worker licenses. Some categories, such as locksmith or alarm installer under supervision, allow applicants as young as 16.
- You cannot be a current member of a police force as defined by the BC Police Act. Peace officers and retired police officers may qualify.
- You must complete identity verification and fingerprinting.

Training:

- Complete the 40 hour Basic Security Training (BST) program through a provider approved by the Justice Institute of British Columbia.
- If you have experience as a Canadian police officer, auxiliary or reserve officer, correctional officer, sheriff, or border services officer, you may qualify for an exemption from BST.

Cost and term:

- The license fee is approximately $100. Fingerprinting and the criminal record check add another $50 to $70.
- The license is valid for five years.
- Processing typically takes 4 to 6 weeks.
- Late renewal triggers a fresh application rather than a simple update, so submit your renewal early.

Even if you hold a valid license from another province, you still need a separate BC license to work in the province.

Québec: Loi sur la sécurité privée (Bureau de la sécurité privée)

Québec regulates security work through the Loi sur la sécurité privée (LSP), administered by the Bureau de la sécurité privée (BSP), created in 2006.

Eligibility requirements:

- You must be at least 18 years old at the time of application.
- You must hold Canadian citizenship, permanent resident status, or a valid Canadian work permit.
- You must have no criminal conviction connected to private security activity, unless you received a pardon.
- You must meet a character and conduct standard evaluated with input from the Sûreté du Québec.

Training:

- Complete a recognized training program of approximately 70 hours total, combining a 54 hour core security course with a 16 hour first aid component.

License term:

- Licenses run on a five year renewal cycle.
- Working with an expired or suspended license is an offence under the LSP and can result in penalties.
- If you work as an independent contractor offering security services, you need both an guard license and an agency license at the same time.

Other Provinces and Territories

Manitoba, Saskatchewan, Nova Scotia, New Brunswick, Newfoundland and Labrador, Prince Edward Island, and the territories each have their own licensing framework. The general pattern holds across all of them:

- A provincial act governs the industry.
- You need a criminal record check.
- You need to complete an approved training course, though required hours vary by province.
- You apply through a provincial registrar or ministry.
- Licenses run on a fixed renewal cycle, typically one to five years.

Contact your provincial ministry of justice or public safety directly for exact requirements, since these details change and smaller provinces update their rules less predictably than Ontario, Alberta, and BC.

License Classes: What Each One Allows

Most provinces separate licenses by activity type. Common classes include:

- **Security guard / security worker.** Covers static guarding, patrol, and access control.
- **Private investigator.** Covers investigation work, often with separate training requirements.
- **Armoured car guard.** Requires use of force and firearms training in provinces that permit armed transport work.
- **Alarm installer / alarm response.** Covers technical installation and monitoring response.
- **Locksmith.** A separate license in most provinces, sometimes bundled with security categories.

Check which class matches the job you want before you enrol in training. Taking the wrong course wastes time and money.

Renewal and Continuing Requirements

Renewal deadlines matter. Missing one often means starting the application process over instead of filing a simple renewal.

Track these dates:

- Your license expiry date.
- Your first aid and CPR expiry date, if your province or employer requires it.
- Any mandatory refresher training tied to your license class.

Set a calendar reminder 60 days before your license expires. Provincial processing times run from a few weeks to over a month, and you cannot legally work on an expired license.

Reciprocity Between Provinces

Canada has no national security license. A license from one province does not automatically work in another. If you move or take a contract in a different province, you need to apply for that province's license, even if your Ontario or Alberta license is still active.

Some provinces give credit for training completed elsewhere. Ask the receiving province's registrar directly whether your existing training hours count toward their requirement before you assume they do.

A Note on Accuracy

Licensing rules change. Several provinces, including Ontario, are actively reviewing their regulations as this book goes to print. Confirm current requirements, fees, and disqualifying offences directly with your provincial registrar before you apply. Do not rely on this section, or any third party guide, as your final source.

Training doesn't end when you get the licence.

Keep learning.
Stay sharp.
Every shift.

SECTION 03

TRAINING AND CERTIFICATIONS

- ☐ Provincial training ☆
- ☐ First Aid / CPR ☆ → Foundation.
- ☐ WHMIS
- ☐ De-escalation
- ☐ Conflict management
- ☐ Crowd management
- ☐ Report writing
- ☐ Use of force (legal)
- ☐ AED
- ☐ Security industry ethics
- ☐ Site-specific training

Foundation.
↓
Keep current.
↓
Apply it.
↓
Get better.

Keep copies of everything.

WHY IT MATTERS

- More knowledge = more confidence
- Better prepared for real situations
- Employers notice initiative
- Builds your reputation

REMEMBER:

- Expiry dates
- Refresher training
- Document everything

TIP:
Set calendar reminders 30 days before expiry.
Don't let it lapse.

TRAIN TODAY.
SAFER TOMORROW.

Good training now → fewer problems later.

Section 3: Training and Certifications

Your basic license training gets you in the door. It does not prepare you for every situation you face on the job. This section covers what training is mandatory, what is optional, and which certifications actually help your career.

Mandatory Basic Training by Province

Every province requires you to complete an approved basic training course before you apply for your license. Hours and content vary.

Province	Course Name	Hours
Ontario	Basic Security Training	40
Alberta	Alberta Basic Security Training (ABST)	40
British Columbia	Basic Security Training (BST)	40
Quebec	BSP-recognized core course	54 (plus 16 hour first aid component)

Course content across provinces covers similar ground: relevant legislation, powers of arrest, use of force law, report writing, communication skills, and emergency response basics. Confirm your course is on your provincial registrar's approved list before you enroll. Unapproved courses will not qualify you for a license, no matter how good the instructor is.

Use of Force Training: What Is Actually Mandatory

This is where guards get confused, so read carefully.

Outside British Columbia, no province in Canada currently mandates a standardized, government certified use of force training program for general security guards. Your basic license course covers use of force law and theory. It does not certify you to carry or use handcuffs, a baton, or pepper spray.

If your job requires you to carry handcuffs or a baton, you need separate, specific training tied to that equipment:

- **Ontario:** Carrying handcuffs or a baton requires completion of Defensive Control Tactics (DCT) training, a two day course covering legal use of force, practical skills testing, and scenario based Judgement and Decision Making Scenarios (JDAS). This is mandatory under the PSISA for any guard authorized by their employer to carry this equipment.

- **Alberta:** Baton and handcuff authorization requires a 40 hour approved training program plus an additional qualification added to your Security Services license. Recertification runs on a shorter course, typically 24 hours, every few years depending on the provider.

- **British Columbia:** BC is the only province with a mandatory provincial standard for advanced use of force training. Advanced Security Training (AST) is a prerequisite for the handcuffing endorsement on your license. The course runs 24 hours, classroom based, and requires renewal every three years.

- **Quebec:** Equipment authorization requirements are set through the BSP and tied to your license category. Confirm current requirements directly with the BSP before carrying any control equipment.

There is no nationally certified "Use of Force Instructor" designation for the private security industry in Canada, apart from BC's provincial standard. Private training companies market their own certifications, and some are well respected in the industry, but a private certificate is not the same as a government mandated credential. Verify that any course you take is accepted by your provincial registrar before you pay for it.

Never carry handcuffs, a baton, or any control equipment without your employer's explicit authorization and the required training. Carrying unauthorized equipment exposes you to criminal liability and puts your license at risk.

First Aid and CPR

Standard First Aid with CPR-C is close to a universal requirement across the industry, even in provinces where it is not written directly into the licensing act. Employers ask for it because incidents happen, and someone on site needs to respond before EMS arrives.

- Certification typically runs for three years before renewal is required.
- Take your recertification course before your card expires. Some employers will not schedule you on shift with an expired certificate.
- Choose a provider recognized by your provincial workers' compensation board. Not all first aid cards carry equal weight with employers.

WHMIS

The Workplace Hazardous Materials Information System (WHMIS) training covers how to identify, handle, and respond to hazardous materials in a workplace. Many security postings, particularly industrial sites, warehouses, and construction sites, require current WHMIS certification before you can work there. The course is short, usually a few hours, and widely available online. Keep your certificate current and bring a copy to any site that asks for it.

Optional Certifications That Boost Employability

These are not required for licensing, but they make you a stronger candidate and often unlock higher paying postings or increases chances for advancement.

- **De-escalation and verbal conflict management training** (such as Verbal Judo or similar programs). Employers value guards who can talk someone down instead of relying on physical intervention.

- **Mental health first aid.** Guards regularly encounter people in crisis. This training gives you a framework for responding safely and appropriately.
- **ASP baton or PPCT style defensive tactics certification.** Even where not mandatory, private certification demonstrates you take physical response seriously and understand liability.
- **Fire warden or fire safety plan training.** Valuable for guards working in high rise buildings, where fire safety plan compliance is a regulatory requirement for the property.
- **Traffic control certification.** Opens up construction site and event postings that pay a premium for flagging and traffic management.
- **Naloxone administration training.** Increasingly relevant for guards working transit, retail, and downtown postings where opioid overdose response has become part of the job in many cities.

Employer Provided vs Self-Funded Training

Some employers cover the cost of your basic license training as a condition of a job offer, especially larger national security companies competing for new hires. Others expect you to arrive already licensed.

Before you pay for training out of pocket, ask a few target employers what they require and what they cover. Paying for a course a specific employer does not need, or that is not accepted in your province, wastes money. If an employer offers to pay for your training, clarify whether that comes with a service commitment. Some companies require you to stay employed for a minimum period or repay training costs if you leave early.

Optional certifications are usually on you to fund, though some employers will reimburse costs once you complete probation or hit a service milestone. Ask directly. It costs nothing to ask and can save you real money.

Continuing Education

Licensing bodies in most provinces require periodic renewal, and some tie renewal to refresher training. Beyond the minimum, treat continuing education as part of building your career, not a box to check.

Guards who invest in de-escalation training, mental health response, and specialized certifications move into supervisor roles, specialized postings, and higher pay brackets faster than guards who do the minimum. Training is one of the few parts of this career you control directly. Use it, the skills you pick up will not only help with advancement, but will make your day to day duties much easier, less stressful and bring you greater enjoyment and fulfillment from your role.

INTERVIEW — 09:00

- ☐ Resume
- ☐ References
- ☐ Licence
- ☐ Arrive early
- ☐ Dress professionally
- ☐ Be prepared
- ☐ Positive attitude

First impressions count.

You're not just being interviewed — you're evaluating them too.

SECTION 04

RESUME AND INTERVIEW TIPS

Know the job.

Understand the site, the role, and the company.

STAR METHOD

S → T → A → R

S	T	A	R
Situation	Task	Action	Result
What was the context?	What was required?	What did YOU do?	What was the outcome?

GIVE EXAMPLES!

COMMON QUESTIONS

- Tell me about yourself.
- Why do you want to work here?
- What are your strengths?
- How do you handle stress or conflict?
- Describe a difficult situation and how you handled it.

TIPS

- Answer honestly.
- Keep answers relevant.
- Speak clearly.
- Stay calm.
- Listen carefully.
- Thank them.

NOTES

- ✓ Confident, not cocky.
- ✓ Professional.
- ✓ Show initiative.
- ✓ Team player.
- ✓ Reliable.

Why should they hire YOU?

REMEMBER: You are selling your value, not just your availability.

Be early.
Not on time — early.

Section 4: Resume and Interview Tips

Your license gets you eligible for the job. Your resume and interview get you hired. Security hiring moves fast in this industry, and employers often fill positions within days of posting. A clear, targeted resume puts you ahead of candidates who send a generic one.

Structuring a Security Resume With No Experience

You do not need prior security experience to build a strong resume. Employers hire new guards constantly. What they look for is reliability, judgment, and a clean record.

Structure your resume in this order:

1. **Contact information.** Name, phone number, email, and city. Leave off your full address.

2. **License status.** State your license number, class, and expiry date at the top, right under your contact information. This is the first thing a hiring manager checks. Make it easy to find.

3. **Summary line.** Two sentences. State your license class, and one or two strengths relevant to the job.

4. **Certifications.** List First Aid/CPR-C, WHMIS, and any use of force or equipment authorization you hold, with expiry dates.

5. **Work experience.** Even without security experience, list jobs that show reliability and public interaction: retail, food service, warehouse, military, or customer-facing roles.

6. **Skills.** Keep this short and specific. Avoid vague terms like "hard worker." Use concrete skills: report writing, conflict de-escalation, CCTV monitoring, access control systems, radio communication.

7. **Availability.** State clearly whether you can work nights, weekends, and on-call shifts. Security scheduling depends heavily on flexibility, and stating this upfront saves everyone time.

Keep the resume to one page if you have under five years of work history. Two pages is acceptable once you have security specific experience to add.

Highlighting Transferable Skills

Employers do not expect every new guard to come from a security background. They look for evidence you can handle the core demands of the job: staying calm, following procedure, and dealing with people.

Match your past experience to these categories:

- **Military or reserve service.** Discipline, chain of command familiarity, and physical readiness translate directly. State your role and rank plainly, without assuming the reader understands military jargon.
- **Retail or customer service.** De-escalating an unhappy customer is close to de-escalating a difficult visitor on a security posting. Say so directly on your resume.
- **Warehouse or logistics.** Familiarity with access control, inventory checks, and physical stamina all transfer well to static and patrol postings.
- **Hospitality.** Front desk or concierge experience maps closely to building concierge security roles. Highlight any experience checking IDs, managing visitor logs, or handling complaints.
- **Volunteer or coaching roles.** Experience supervising groups, especially youth or large crowds, shows employers you can manage a scene and communicate authority calmly.

Whatever your background, connect it explicitly to the job. Do not assume the hiring manager will make the connection for you.

Common Interview Questions and Strong Answers

Security interviews are usually short and practical. Employers want to see how you think under pressure, not memorized textbook answers.

"Why do you want to work in security?" Give a real reason. Avoid generic lines like "I like helping people." A strong answer names something specific: stable shift work, interest in a law enforcement career path, or a genuine interest in the responsibility of the role.

"How would you handle an aggressive or intoxicated person on site?" Walk through a clear sequence: assess the situation from a safe distance, use calm and direct verbal communication, avoid physical contact unless necessary for safety, and call for backup or police if the situation escalates. Employers want to hear that you prioritize de-escalation and safety over confrontation.

"Describe a time you had to make a decision without a supervisor available." Use a real example, even from a non-security job. Employers care about your decision making process more than the specific outcome.

"What would you do if you saw a coworker breaking policy?" Employers want honesty here. State that you would report it through the correct channel, not confront the coworker directly or ignore it.

"Are you comfortable working nights, weekends, or alone on a site?" Answer honestly. Overstating your availability to get hired backfires quickly once the schedule doesn't match your real limits.

"How do you handle boredom during a slow shift?" Employers ask this because slow shifts are common and guards who cannot handle downtime become a liability. Talk about staying alert through regular patrol checks, log reviews, and maintaining focus even when nothing is happening.

Questions to Ask the Employer

Asking good questions shows you are serious about the job and helps you avoid a bad fit.

- What type of site will I be working, and what does a typical shift look like?
- Is training paid, and is it provided before my first solo shift?

- What equipment will I be authorized to carry, and is that training included?
- What is the process if I need backup or police assistance on site?
- How is overtime and shift coverage handled?
- Is there a path to supervisor or specialized postings within the company?

Red Flags in a Job Posting

Watch for these warning signs before you apply or accept an offer:

- No mention of a license requirement. Legitimate employers state this clearly.
- Pay significantly below the provincial average with no explanation.
- Vague job descriptions that do not specify the site type or duties.
- Pressure to start before your license or background check is complete.
- No mention of training, equipment, or safety procedures.

A legitimate security employer wants a properly licensed, trained guard on site. A company cutting corners on licensing or training is a company that will cut corners on your safety too.

Following Up After an Interview

Send a short thank you message within 24 hours. Keep it brief: thank the interviewer for their time, restate your interest in the role, and mention your availability to start. This step is simple, and most candidates skip it. It costs you five minutes and sets you apart.

If you have not heard back within the timeline the employer gave you, a single polite follow up is appropriate. Do not follow up more than once before that timeline passes.

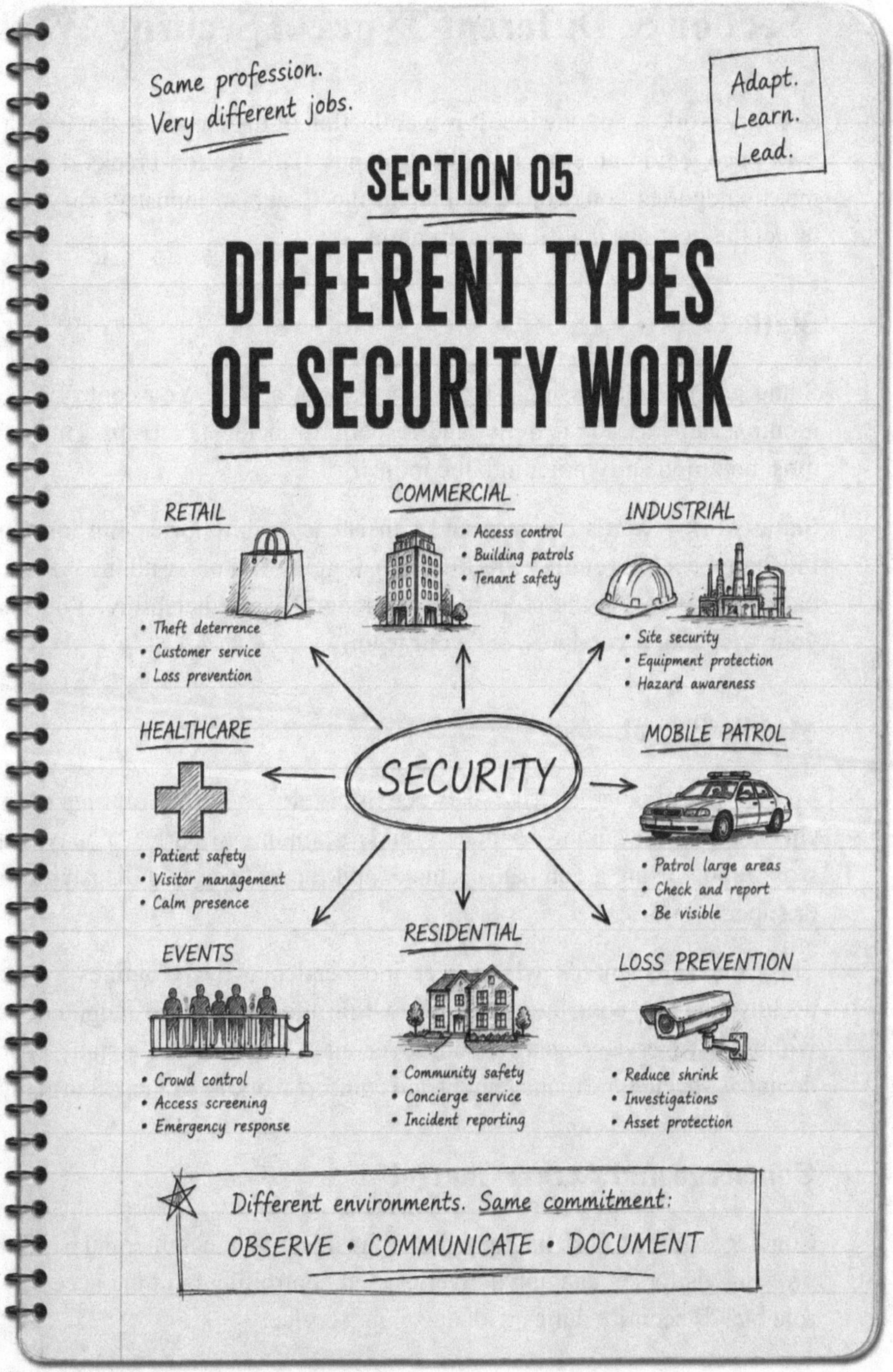
Same profession.
Very different jobs.
Adapt.
Learn.
Lead.
SECTION 05
DIFFERENT TYPES OF SECURITY WORK
RETAIL
• Theft deterrence
• Customer service
• Loss prevention
COMMERCIAL
• Access control
• Building patrols
• Tenant safety
INDUSTRIAL
• Site security
• Equipment protection
• Hazard awareness
HEALTHCARE
• Patient safety
• Visitor management
• Calm presence
SECURITY
MOBILE PATROL
• Patrol large areas
• Check and report
• Be visible
EVENTS
• Crowd control
• Access screening
• Emergency response
RESIDENTIAL
• Community safety
• Concierge service
• Incident reporting
LOSS PREVENTION
• Reduce shrink
• Investigations
• Asset protection
Different environments. Same commitment:
OBSERVE • COMMUNICATE • DOCUMENT

Section 5: Different Types of Security Work

Security work is not one job. It is a collection of distinct roles, each with its own pace, environment, and skill demands. This section breaks down the main categories you will encounter in the Canadian industry, so you can target the postings that fit your strengths.

Static Guard

Static guards work a single fixed location for a shift. You control access, monitor cameras, log activity, and respond to incidents on site. This is the most common entry point into the industry.

Static work rewards patience and consistency. Shifts often run long, and much of the job is routine: checking IDs, logging visitors, walking scheduled patrol routes inside the property. The tradeoff is predictability. You know your site, your procedures, and your team.

Mobile Patrol

Mobile patrol guards drive between multiple properties during a shift, checking locks, walking perimeters, and responding to alarms. You typically work alone, using a company vehicle, and report back to a dispatch center or supervisor.

This role suits guards who prefer independence over routine. You can usually manage your own schedule within the shift, make judgment calls without a supervisor nearby, and cover more ground than a static post. It demands strong time management and comfort working alone, often at night.

Concierge and Access Control

Concierge guards work the front desk of residential or commercial buildings, greeting visitors, managing deliveries, and controlling building access. This role blends security duties with customer service.

Tenants and residents interact with concierge guards daily, so communication skills matter as much as security training here. You need to be firm on access control while staying approachable. Buildings with a concierge desk often expect a polished, professional presentation, including grooming and uniform standards above a typical static post.

Retail Loss Prevention

Loss prevention guards work inside retail stores, watching for theft, often in plain clothes rather than uniform. You observe customer behavior, review camera footage, and intervene when you have grounds to believe theft is occurring.

This role requires restraint and legal knowledge. You need to understand your citizen's arrest powers precisely, since a wrongful detention exposes you and your employer to legal liability. Loss prevention guards typically receive specific training on store policy, evidence documentation, and safe intervention procedures beyond the basic license course.

Event Security

Event security guards manage crowds, check tickets, screen bags, and handle disputes at concerts, sporting events, and festivals. Shifts are often short and high energy, with a large team working together under a site supervisor.

This role suits guards who work well in teams and stay calm in high noise, high density environments. Crowd management skills matter more here than in almost any other posting. You need to read a crowd, spot problems early, and communicate clearly over radio in a loud environment.

Corporate and Executive Protection

Executive protection agents provide close protection for high profile individuals: executives, celebrities, or public figures. This is a specialized field that typically requires years of experience, advanced training, and often a background in law enforcement or military service.

Corporate security guards, a related but distinct role, protect office buildings, monitor employee and visitor access, and often work alongside a company's internal risk or facilities team. This path offers more stability and a clearer route into corporate security management for guards who want to move up without pursuing close protection work specifically.

Industrial and Construction Site Security

Guards on industrial and construction sites protect equipment, materials, and the site perimeter, often during off hours when the site is unstaffed by regular workers. Theft of tools, fuel, and copper wiring is a constant risk on active construction sites, making this a high vigilance posting.

This work often happens outdoors in all weather conditions. WHMIS certification is commonly required, since these sites involve hazardous materials. Some postings require comfort working nights alone on a large, dark property.

Healthcare Security

Hospital and healthcare security guards manage access control, respond to patient behavioral incidents, and support staff during emergencies. This role increasingly requires specific de-escalation and mental health response training, since a significant portion of incidents involve patients in crisis rather than criminal activity.

Healthcare postings often pay above average for entry level work because of the specialized skill set required. Guards who pursue mental health first aid training stand out strongly for these roles.

Cannabis Retail Security

Legal cannabis retail stores in Canada are regulated provincially, and most provinces require licensed security personnel on site, particularly given the cash volumes these stores handle. In Ontario, for example, the Alcohol and Gaming Commission of Ontario (AGCO) sets compliance conditions for retail cannabis stores that include safety and security requirements as part of store licensing.

Guards in this posting handle age verification, queue management, cash handling awareness, and loss prevention specific to cannabis retail. Expect employer specific training on product regulations and ID verification procedures on top of your provincial license.

Armored Transport

Armored transport guards move cash and valuables between banks, retailers, and processing centers. This is one of the higher paying entry points into the industry, but it comes with the highest risk profile and the strictest training requirements, including use of force and firearms training where permitted.

This role typically requires additional licensing beyond a standard security worker license, a clean record with no exceptions, credit check and often a minimum period of general security experience before a company will consider you for the position.

Alarm Response

Alarm response guards patrol on an on-call basis, responding to triggered alarms at client properties. You investigate the cause, secure the property if needed, and coordinate with police if there is evidence of a break in.

This role demands fast, independent judgment. You often arrive at a property alone, at night, with no idea whether the alarm is a false trigger or an active break in in progress. Guards in this posting need strong situational awareness and clear protocols for when to enter a property versus when to wait for police.

Choosing the Right Posting for You

Match the posting to your strengths, not just the pay rate. A guard who thrives on independence will burn out fast in a high interaction concierge role. A guard who enjoys people will find static overnight patrol tedious. Try different posting types early in your career if your employer allows it.

Knowing which environment suits you will shape a much stronger, longer career than chasing the highest hourly rate on your first job.

Radio check.

- Know your channel
- Test your radio
- Keep it simple

> Good radio practice saves time — and prevents errors.

SECTION 06

THE PHONETIC ALPHABET AND RADIO ETIQUETTE

A - ALPHA	N - NOVEMBER
B - BRAVO	O - OSCAR
C - CHARLIE	P - PAPA
D - DELTA	Q - QUEBEC
E - ECHO	R - ROMEO
F - FOXTROT	S - SIERRA
G - GOLF	T - TANGO
H - HOTEL	U - UNIFORM
I - INDIA	V - VICTOR
J - JULIETT	W - WHISKEY
K - KILO	X - X-RAY
L - LIMA	Y - YANKEE
M - MIKE	Z - ZULU

THINK → KEY → PAUSE → SPEAK

1. Think about what you need to say.
2. Key the microphone.
3. Pause... let others finish.
4. Speak clearly and concisely.
5. Release the microphone.

EXAMPLE:

"Control, this is Unit 12. On patrol at Main Entrance. All quiet."

KEEP IT PROFESSIONAL.

- ✓ Use plain language.
- ✓ Avoid codes unless trained.
- ✓ No personal conversations.
- ✓ No unnecessary transmissions.
- ✓ Listen as much as you speak.

GOOD RADIO HABITS

- Be brief.
- Be clear.
- Be accurate.
- Be polite.
- Be professional. ☆

☆ COMMON TERMS:

10-4 = Affirmative (OK / Understood)
10-20 = Location
10-23 = Arrived on scene
10-97 = En route
10-8 = In service
10-7 = Out of service

REMEMBER:

CLEAR • SHORT • PROFESSIONAL

Good radio practice = Good teamwork.

Poor radio practice = confusion and delays.

When in doubt, ask.

Section 6: The Phonetic Alphabet and Radio Etiquette

Your radio is one of the most important tools you carry. Used well, it keeps you safe, keeps your team coordinated, and keeps a scene under control. Used poorly, it creates confusion at exactly the moment clarity matters most. This section covers the phonetic alphabet, the etiquette that makes radio communication work, and the ten codes you may encounter on the job.

The Full NATO Phonetic Alphabet

This is the international standard used by security, police, fire, aviation, and military communications worldwide. Learn it exactly as written below. Do not substitute your own words.

Letter	**Code Word**	**Letter**	**Code Word**
A	Alpha	N	November
B	Bravo	O	Oscar
C	Charlie	P	Papa
D	Delta	Q	Quebec
E	Echo	R	Romeo
F	Foxtrot	S	Sierra
G	Golf	T	Tango
H	Hotel	U	Uniform
I	India	V	Victor
J	Juliett	W	Whiskey
K	Kilo	X	X-ray
L	Lima	Y	Yankee
M	Mike	Z	Zulu

Note the spelling of Juliett with two T's and Alpha with an "f" rather than "ph." These are the official spellings used in international radio protocol, designed to avoid confusion regardless of accent or language background.

Numbers Over Radio

Say each digit individually rather than as a full number. "One five" is clearer over radio than "fifteen," which can sound like "fifty" through static or a weak signal. Some sites use "niner" instead of "nine," to avoid confusion with "five" over poor audio. Check your site's specific conventions.

Why the Phonetic Alphabet Matters

A license plate, a unit number, or a last name becomes unreliable over radio without a shared standard. "B" and "D" sound almost identical through static. The phonetic alphabet removes that risk, because each code word sounds distinct even under poor conditions. This matters most exactly when clarity matters most: relaying a description to police, confirming a unit number during an emergency, or reading out a plate during an active incident.

Radio Etiquette and Procedures

Knowing the alphabet and the codes is only half the skill. How you use the radio matters just as much as what you say into it.

Keying up correctly. Press the transmit button a half second before you start speaking. Radios often clip the first syllable if you speak the instant you press the button. Wait for the tone or the brief pause before talking, and hold the button down for your entire transmission, releasing only once you are finished.

Think before you transmit. Plan your sentence before you key up. A long, rambling transmission blocks the channel for everyone else, including someone who might need to report a real emergency. State your call sign, then your message, in the shortest clear form possible.

One speaker at a time. If two people key up at once, both transmissions get lost or garbled together. Listen for a clear pause before you transmit, especially during a busy incident when multiple guards want to report at once. If you hear another transmission start as you key up, release immediately and wait.

Confirm every message. Silence does not confirm receipt. Always respond with a clear "copy" or "received" when you get an instruction. If you are unsure whether your own message went through, ask directly: "Did you copy?" Do not assume the other party heard you just because you said it.

Use call signs, not names. Most sites assign call signs (Post 1, Unit 3, Base) instead of first names. This keeps communication professional, consistent, and protects guard identity on a channel others might overhear.

Close every transmission clearly. End with "over" if you expect a reply, or "out" if the exchange is finished. This tells the other party exactly whether you are waiting on them or done talking.

Keep a professional tone at all times. Assume anyone could be listening to your channel, including a supervisor, a client, or someone with a scanner. Stay factual and calm, even during a stressful call.

Test your radio at the start of every shift. Confirm your battery level, your volume, and that you can reach base or your supervisor before you rely on the radio in an emergency. Finding out your radio is dead during an incident is too late.

Know your dead zones. Stairwells, elevators, underground parking, and certain corners of large buildings often have poor radio reception. Learn where these are on your site before you need to communicate from one, and have a backup plan, such as a cell phone number, for those areas.

Ten Codes: What They Are and How to Use Them

Ten codes are a shorthand system, originally developed for police radio use, where a number following "10" represents a specific standard message. Some security companies, particularly older or larger firms, still use them. Plain language has become the more common standard across Canadian policing and much of private security, since ten codes are not consistent between agencies and regions, and confusion between departments using different code sets has caused real problems during joint responses.

Learn your specific employer's protocol before assuming either system applies. If your company uses ten codes, here are commonly recognized examples and how they are typically used on shift:

Code	Meaning	Example Use
10-4	Acknowledged / message received	"10-4, heading to Post 2 now."
10-7	Out of service	"Unit 3, 10-7 for a break, back in 15."
10-8	In service / available	"Unit 3, 10-8, back on patrol."
10-9	Repeat your last message	"Base, 10-9, you were breaking up."
10-13	Advise weather or road conditions	"Base, 10-13, parking lot is icing up."
10-19	Return to base or station	"Unit 2, 10-19, come back to the office."
10-20	Location / state your location	"Base to Unit 3, what's your 10-20?"
10-33	Emergency, all units stand by	"10-33, need immediate backup at the loading dock."
10-97	Arrived at scene	"Unit 4, 10-97 at the north entrance."
10-99	Situation resolved / mission complete	"Base, 10-99, subject has left the property."

Important cautions about ten codes:

- These meanings are common, but not universal. A "10-20" at one company might mean something different at another. Never assume a code you learned at a previous job carries over to a new employer without confirming first.
- If you work alongside police or fire on a regular basis, plain language avoids the risk of a code mismatch during a joint response. When in doubt, say it in plain words.
- Never rely on a ten code during a genuine emergency if there is any chance the other party might misunderstand it. "I need backup now" is always understood. A garbled or misremembered code is not.

Site Specific Codes

Beyond ten codes, many sites use their own shorthand for common situations. Examples you might encounter:

- **Code Green:** All clear, no issues.
- **Code Yellow:** Minor incident, situation under control.
- **Code Red:** Active emergency, immediate response needed.
- **Code Adam:** Missing or lost child, common in malls and large retail sites.
- **Signal 100:** Officer or guard needs immediate assistance, drop everything.

These codes are not standardized across the industry. A "Code Red" at one site might mean fire, and at another it might mean an active threat. Learn your specific site's codes during onboarding, and never assume a code from a previous job carries over to a new employer.

What to Do When Radios Fail

Radios fail. Batteries die, signals drop in stairwells or underground parking, and equipment breaks. Have a plan before it happens, not during an emergency.

- **Carry a charged spare battery or backup radio if your site allows it.** A dead radio during an incident leaves you isolated.
- **Know your site's dead zones.** Stairwells, elevators, underground levels, and certain corners of large buildings often have poor radio reception. Know where these are before you need to communicate from one.
- **Have a backup communication method.** A cell phone with your supervisor's direct number saved is the most common backup. Confirm this is acceptable under your site's procedures.

- **Establish a check in protocol.** Some sites require guards to check in at set intervals. If a scheduled check in is missed, that itself becomes a signal that something may be wrong. Know your site's protocol and follow it exactly.
- **If your radio fails during an active incident, move toward help physically if you cannot restore communication quickly.** Getting a message to someone matters more than staying at your exact post if you cannot otherwise reach anyone.

Sample Radio Call Scripts

Routine check-in: "Base, this is Post 2, all clear, over."

Reporting a suspicious person: "Base, this is Post 1. I have a suspicious individual near the east entrance, dark jacket, appears to be attempting to access a restricted door. Requesting backup, over."

Reporting a medical emergency: "Base, this is Unit 3. Medical emergency in the main lobby, one individual unresponsive. Requesting EMS immediately, over."

Requesting immediate assistance: "Base, this is Post 4. I need immediate backup at the loading dock. Repeat, immediate backup, over."

Confirming an instruction: "Base, copy that, proceeding to check the north stairwell, over."

Ending a transmission cleanly: Always close with "over" if you expect a reply, or "out" if the conversation is finished. This tells the other party clearly whether you are waiting for a response.

Building Radio Fluency

Fluency with the phonetic alphabet, your site's codes, and clean radio etiquette comes from repetition, not memorization the night before a test.

Drill 1: Spell your own name and site address using the phonetic alphabet, without hesitating on any letter.

Drill 2: Practice a full radio call, start to finish. For example: "Base, this is Post 4, reporting a suspicious vehicle, plate reads Bravo, Charlie, Kilo, one nine seven, requesting a check, over." Run this until it feels automatic under pressure, not just in a quiet room.

Drill 3: Review your employer's code list, if they use one, until you can recall the common codes without checking a card.

Drill 4: Listen closely to experienced guards and supervisors on the radio. Notice how they phrase transmissions, and model your own calls after theirs.

Clean, confident radio communication is one of the fastest ways to build credibility with your team, your supervisor, and any police or fire crews you work alongside during a real incident. Keep a printed reference card, covering both the phonetic alphabet and your site's specific codes, in your uniform pocket or vehicle until all of it becomes second nature.

Building the Habit

Radio skills fade without practice. Use your slow shifts to run through call scripts mentally, and pay close attention to how experienced guards and supervisors phrase their transmissions. Clean, confident radio communication is one of the fastest ways to build credibility with your team and with the police or fire crews you may need to work alongside during a real incident.

Remember:

- Facts – not opinions.
- Be objective.
- Write clearly.
- Use proper grammar.

☆ What you write today could be read in court tomorrow.

SECTION 07

REPORT WRITING

WHO?	Involved parties, witnesses, staff, unit numbers.
WHAT?	Exact details of what happened.
WHEN?	Date and time.
WHERE?	Specific location.
WHY?	Reason or cause (if known).
HOW?	How it happened.

REPORT CHECKLIST

- ☐ Accurate
- ☐ Complete
- ☐ Chronological
- ☐ Clear & concise
- ☐ Professional
- ☐ Proofread ☆

EXAMPLE TIMESTAMP:

23:17 hrs

→ Use 24-hour time.

NOTES:

- Use exact words spoken.
- Write in chronological order.
- Include actions taken.
- Attach photos, video, or diagrams if available.

Be precise. Small details matter.

BE OBJECTIVE – NOT SUBJECTIVE

DON'T WRITE:

"~~The subject was rude and aggressive.~~"

⇒

WRITE:

"The subject raised his voice and stated, 'I'm not leaving.'"

REPORT STRUCTURE

1. Introduction
2. Narrative (chronological)
3. Actions taken
4. Statements (quotes)
5. Conclusion
6. Attachments / evidence

FINAL REMINDER

Your report may be the only account of what happened.

MAKE IT COUNT.

Professional reports reflect a professional guard.

Section 7: Report Writing

Your report is the only record of what happened after your shift ends. Memory fades. People change their story. A well written report protects you, your employer, and the truth. This is one of the most important skills in this job, and it gets less attention than it deserves.

Why Report Quality Protects You Legally

If an incident on your site ends up in court, your report becomes evidence. Police, lawyers, and insurance adjusters may read it months or years after the event. A vague or sloppy report weakens your credibility as a witness. A clear, factual report backs up your account and protects you from liability.

Poor reports create real problems:

- A vague description of an incident can be read as an admission of negligence.
- Missing details make it impossible to verify your account later.
- Sloppy writing damages your credibility if you testify in court.
- Inconsistent reports, compared across shifts, raise doubt about what actually happened.

Treat every report as a document someone else will scrutinize closely, because eventually, one might.

Structure of a Solid Incident Report

A strong report follows a consistent structure. Use this format every time so nothing gets missed.

1. **Header information.** Date, time, your name and badge or license number, site name, and shift.

2. **Location.** The exact location of the incident. Be specific: not "parking lot," but "north parking lot, row 3, near the loading dock entrance."

3. **Persons involved.** Names if known, physical descriptions if not, and their role in the incident (witness, subject, victim).

4. **Chronological account.** What happened, in the order it happened. Use timestamps where possible.

5. **Actions taken.** What you did in response: called police, provided first aid, contacted a supervisor, and so on.

6. **Outcome.** How the situation resolved by the end of your report.

7. **Signature and time completed.** Sign and date the report, noting when you wrote it relative to the incident.

Write your report as close to the incident as possible. Details fade fast, and a report written hours later loses accuracy even with good intentions.

Facts vs Opinion

This is the single most common mistake in security report writing. Stick to what you observed. Leave out what you assume.

Fact: "The individual raised their voice and stepped toward the front desk." **Opinion:** "The individual was clearly trying to intimidate the staff member."

Fact: "The individual smelled of alcohol and had difficulty standing without support." **Opinion:** "The individual was drunk."

You can describe what you observed that led to a conclusion, but avoid stating the conclusion as fact unless it is confirmed (a breathalyzer result, a medical diagnosis, a police finding). Describe behavior, not your interpretation of intent or mental state. A defense lawyer will pick apart any report that states conclusions your observations do not directly support.

What to include:

- Direct observations: what you saw, heard, and did.

- Exact quotes when possible, in quotation marks.
- Times, measurements, and specific locations.
- Names of witnesses and how to reach them if known.

What to leave out:

- Assumptions about motive or intent.
- Second hand information you did not personally witness, unless clearly labeled as such ("Witness stated that...").
- Personal opinions about the individuals involved.
- Speculation about what might have happened before or after your observation.

Sample Completed Reports

Sample 1: Patrol Report

Date: March 14, 2026 Time: 22:15 Guard: J. Thompson, License #A1234567 Site: Meridian Business Park, Building C

22:00 - Began scheduled patrol of Building C, floors 1 through 4. 22:04 - Checked and confirmed all fire exits on floor 1 secure and unobstructed. 22:09 - Noted exterior light out at rear loading dock entrance. Logged for maintenance follow up. 22:15 - Completed patrol. All doors checked and secure. No incidents to report.

Signed: J. Thompson Report completed: 22:20

Sample 2: Incident Report

Date: March 14, 2026 Time: 23:40 Guard: J. Thompson, License #A1234567 Site: Meridian Business Park, Building C, main lobby

At approximately 23:35, I observed an unknown individual, approximately 30-40 years old, wearing a grey hooded sweatshirt, attempting to open the locked door to the server room on floor 2. I approached and asked the individual to identify themself and state their business. The individual stated they were "just looking for the bathroom" and left the area, walking toward the east stairwell.

I followed at a distance and observed the individual exit the building through the east stairwell door at 23:38. I did not physically intervene, as the individual left the property without further incident. I contacted my supervisor, M. Reyes, at 23:40 to report the incident. I reviewed the lobby camera footage covering the timeframe and confirmed the individual entered through the main lobby at 23:20 without signing in at the front desk.

Action taken: Reported incident to supervisor. Flagged camera footage for retention. Recommended review of front desk sign in enforcement during evening hours.

Signed: J. Thompson Report completed: 23:55

Sample 3: Use of Force Report

Date: March 14, 2026 Time: 20:10 Guard: J. Thompson, License #A1234567 Site: Riverside Mall, Food Court entrance

At 20:05, I responded to a report from mall staff of an individual, later identified as [name redacted], refusing to leave after being asked twice by staff to stop panhandling near the food court entrance. Upon my arrival, the individual was standing near the entrance, raised their voice, and stated "I'm not going anywhere." I informed them that they were trespassing on private property and asked them to leave.

The individual took a step toward me and raised their right arm. I stepped back and placed my hand on their shoulder to redirect them toward the exit. The individual did not resist further and walked out of the building at my direction. No handcuffs, baton, or additional force was used. I did not sustain injury. The individual did not appear injured.

I contacted my supervisor, M. Reyes, immediately following the incident at 20:12. Mall security camera footage from the food court entrance was flagged for retention covering 20:00 to 20:15.

Signed: J. Thompson Report completed: 20:30

Common Errors That Weaken a Report

Vague time references. "Later that evening" means nothing months later. Use exact times or specific time durations whenever you can.

Missing witness information. If someone saw the incident, get their name and contact information at the time. You cannot go back and find them later.

Editorializing. Phrases like "the suspect was clearly guilty" or "they were obviously lying" weaken your credibility. Stick to observed behavior.

Passive, unclear writing. "The door was found open" tells the reader nothing about who found it or when. Write "I found the door open at 22:04" instead.

Skipping the outcome. A report that ends mid incident, without stating how it was resolved, leaves an open question that undermines the entire document.

Inconsistent terminology. If you refer to the same person as "the individual" in one paragraph and "the suspect" in another, it creates confusion about whether you mean the same person.

Digital Reporting Tools

Many security companies now use digital reporting platforms instead of paper forms. These tools often include timestamped photo attachments, GPS location tagging, and templates that prompt you for required fields. Common platforms in the Canadian industry include Trackforce Valiant, Guard1, and various company specific apps.

Digital tools reduce the risk of missing required information, since templates prompt you field by field. They also create a searchable, timestamped record that is harder to dispute later. Learn your employer's specific platform thoroughly during onboarding. A report saved incorrectly or submitted late defeats the purpose of the tool.

Regardless of the platform, the underlying skill is the same: write clearly, stick to facts, and complete your report while the details are still fresh.

Real experience.
Earned the hard way.

No two shifts are the same.

SECTION 08

TIPS FOR ON THE JOB

Stay alert.
Stay humble.
Stay professional.

THINGS THEY DON'T TEACH YOU

- ★ Know where the washrooms are.
- ★ Learn everyone's name.
- ★ Carry two pens.
- ★ Keep a small notepad.
- ★ Check your equipment BEFORE patrol.
- ★ Read the site post orders — really read them.
- ★ Don't just watch cameras — observe.
- ★ Report small issues before they get big.
- ★ Never assume the last shift handled it.
- ★ Keep your phone for emergencies only.
- ★ Be visible. Be approachable.
- ★ Follow through on what you say you'll do.

YOUR GEAR

- ☐ Radio (charged)
- ☐ Flashlight
- ☐ Notepad
- ☐ Keys / Access
- ☐ ID & Licence
- ☐ First Aid basics
- ☐ Two pens ✓

People notice the little things.

If something feels wrong — investigate.

THINGS TO REMEMBER

- You are the eyes and ears.
- Documentation protects everyone.
- Calm is contagious.
- Stay in your lane.
- Ask questions.
- If you don't know — find out.

DAILY CHECK

- ☐ Uniform / appearance
- ☐ Equipment
- ☐ Radio check
- ☐ Post orders
- ☐ Site hazards
- ☐ Mindset

Good habits = Good shifts

Your attitude sets the tone for the shift.

At the end of the day...

- ✓ Did you keep people safe?
- ✓ Did you follow policy?
- ✓ Did you document the facts?
- ✓ Could you have done anything better?

→ Learn. Improve. Repeat.

★ Take pride. Take responsibility. Take care of each other.

Section 8: Tips for on the Job

Training teaches you procedure. Experience teaches you judgment. This section covers the practical habits that separate a solid guard from a guard who is just showing up. None of this replaces your training. It builds on it.

Situational Awareness Basics

Situational awareness means noticing what is normal on your site, so you notice fast when something is not. This skill develops with time, but you can speed it up deliberately with effort.

- **Learn your site's baseline.** Know who normally comes and goes, what times are busy, what vehicles regularly park where. A pattern break, like an unfamiliar car parked in the same spot for hours, stands out only if you know what normal looks like.
- **Scan, do not stare.** Keep your eyes moving across your environment instead of fixing on one spot or one screen. Threats and problems often start at the edge of your attention, not the center.
- **Position yourself with visibility.** Stand or sit where you can see entrances, exits, and the main areas of activity. Avoid positioning yourself with your back to the room for long stretches.
- **Trust the small feeling that something is off.** Guards develop instinct over time. If something feels wrong before you can articulate why, pay closer attention rather than dismissing the feeling.
- **Avoid distraction traps.** Phones, personal conversations, and prolonged focus on one task (like paperwork) create blind spots. Handle these during appropriate breaks, not during active monitoring periods.

De-escalation Before Confrontation

Most conflicts you face do not require physical intervention. They require calm, clear communication before things get worse.

- **Lower your voice, not raise it.** Speaking calmly and quietly often draws someone's attention and de-escalates faster than matching their volume.
- **Give people space.** Standing too close to an agitated person increases tension. Keep a reasonable distance, especially early in an interaction.
- **Use simple, direct language.** Avoid long explanations when someone is agitated. Short, clear statements are easier to process under stress: "I need you to step back," not a lengthy justification.
- **Offer a way out.** Where possible, give the person a face saving option to comply: "Let's head toward the exit together" works better than a blunt order in many situations.
- **Know when de-escalation is not working.** If a situation is clearly escalating despite your efforts, disengage to a safe distance and call for backup rather than continuing to push a failing approach.

Documenting Everything

If it is not written down, it did not happen, at least as far as anyone reviewing the incident later is concerned. Build the habit of logging details as they happen, not from memory at the end of a shift.

- Keep a notebook or your digital reporting tool accessible at all times, not locked in an office or vehicle.
- Log unusual observations immediately, even minor ones. A pattern only becomes visible if individual entries exist to compare.
- Note times precisely. "Around 9" is far less useful than "09:03."

- If you are ever unsure whether something is worth logging, then it is. A short, unnecessary note costs nothing. A missing note on something that mattered can cost you credibility later.

Building Rapport With Tenants, Staff, and the Public

Guards who build genuine rapport with the people on their site get better cooperation, better information, and fewer conflicts overall.

- Learn names where appropriate. Tenants and regular staff notice and appreciate a guard who remembers them.
- Be consistent in tone and professionalism, whether you are talking to a building executive or a janitor. People notice inconsistency, and it damages trust.
- Answer questions patiently, even repetitive ones. You may have answered "where's the washroom" fifty times today. It is the first time for this person.
- Stay approachable without becoming overly familiar. Friendliness supports your authority. Being too casual undermines it.

Good rapport pays off directly. Staff and tenants who trust you are far more likely to report suspicious activity, tip you off to a problem before it escalates, and back up your account if an incident occurs.

Staying Alert During Slow Shifts

Boredom is one of the most underrated risks in this job. A guard who mentally checks out during a quiet stretch is a guard who misses the moment something actually happens.

- Keep moving. Patrols break up long stretches of stillness and keep you physically and mentally engaged.
- Vary your routine within policy. Walking the same exact path at the same exact time every hour makes you predictable to anyone watching, and it dulls your own attention.

- Use downtime productively. Review site procedures, catch up on paperwork, or run phonetic alphabet drills. Idle time spent on your phone is time your attention is not on the site.
- Set mental check in points. Every 15-30 minutes, consciously reassess your surroundings rather than letting hours pass on autopilot.

Personal Safety Habits

Your safety matters as much as the property or people you are protecting. No incident report is worth an injury that could have been avoided.

- Always know your nearest exits and your backup options before you need them.
- Do not enter an unclear or potentially dangerous situation alone if backup is available. Wait for support unless someone's immediate safety requires action.
- Keep your equipment (flashlight, radio, phone) charged and on you at all times, not left in a vehicle or office.
- Trust your training and your instincts equally. If a situation feels unsafe, treat it as unsafe, even if you cannot immediately explain why.
- Take care of your physical health outside of work. Long shifts and irregular hours take a toll. Sleep, hydration, and basic fitness directly affect your alertness and judgment on the job.

The Common Thread

Every tip in this section comes back to the same idea: pay attention, stay calm, and write it down. These three habits, practiced consistently, will carry you further in this career than any single piece of equipment or certification.

Protect life first.

- ☆ Stay calm.
- ☆ Assess quickly.
- ☆ Act safely.
- ☆ Communicate clearly.

Preparation prevents panic.

SECTION 09

FIRE, GAS LEAKS, BOMB THREATS, AND OTHER EMERGENCY PLANNING AND RESPONSE

☆ Know your building. Know your plan.

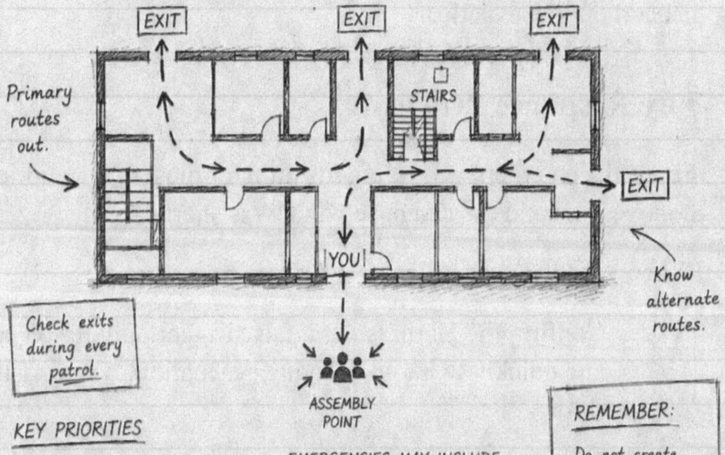

Check exits during every patrol.

KEY PRIORITIES

- ☐ Protect life
- ☐ Call emergency services
- ☐ Contain the situation (if safe)
- ☐ Account for people
- ☐ Document everything

EMERGENCIES MAY INCLUDE:

- Fire / Smoke
- Gas Leak
- Bomb Threat
- Medical Emergency
- Severe Weather
- Active Threat
- Other Critical Incidents

REMEMBER:

Do not create another casualty.

You are there to help — not to become a victim.

IMPORTANT:

Follow your site emergency plan.
If you are unsure — ask.
If you are in danger — get out.
Call for help.

PLAN.

A good plan protects everyone.

Section 9: Fire, Gas Leaks, Bomb Threats, and Other Emergency Planning and Response

Emergencies do not wait for you to feel ready. Your response in the first two minutes of a fire, a gas leak, or a threat call often shapes the outcome more than anything that happens afterward. This section covers the core protocols every guard needs to know before an emergency happens.

Every site has its own emergency plan, developed for that specific building and its risks. What follows is the general framework. Learn your site specific plan in detail during onboarding, and know it does not always match this general outline exactly.

Fire Response Protocols

Fire is the emergency most guards train for most often, and for good reason: it moves fast and the response window is short.

When you discover a fire or a fire alarm activates:

1. Confirm the alarm is not a false trigger only if you can do so safely and quickly, without delaying evacuation. Never assume an alarm is false.

2. Activate the building alarm system if it has not already triggered.

3. Call 911 immediately, even if you believe the fire department has already been automatically notified through a monitored system. Confirm the call went through.

4. Begin or support evacuation according to your site's fire safety plan. Know your building's evacuation routes and muster points before an alarm ever sounds.

5. Direct people away from elevators. Elevators must not be used during a fire evacuation.

6. Assist anyone with mobility limitations according to your site's plan for persons requiring evacuation assistance. Many high rise buildings have designated refuge areas and specific procedures for this.

7. Do not re-enter the building once evacuated, and do not allow others to re-enter, until fire department personnel confirm it is safe.

8. Meet arriving fire crews at the main entrance if possible, and provide them with any information you have: location of the fire, number of people still inside if known, and any hazards you are aware of.

If you are trained and certified as a building fire warden, follow your specific fire safety plan procedures, which may include closing fire doors, checking specific floors, or operating fire panel controls. Do not attempt fire panel operations without training.

Gas Leak Procedures

A suspected gas leak requires immediate, careful action. Natural gas is highly flammable, and the wrong response can turn a leak into an explosion.

If you smell gas or suspect a leak:

1. Do not use any electrical switch, including light switches, elevators, or two way radios, inside the affected area. A spark can ignite a gas leak.

2. Evacuate the immediate area calmly, without creating panic that could cause people to rush and cause injury.

3. Once safely outside the affected area, call your local gas utility emergency line and 911.

4. Do not attempt to locate or fix the source of the leak yourself.

5. Keep people away from the area until the utility company or fire department confirms it is safe.

6. If you used a radio before realizing there was a gas concern, move well away from the area before making any further radio calls.

Know the location of your site's gas shutoff valve for reference, but only utility personnel or trained maintenance staff should operate it, unless your specific site procedures state otherwise.

Bomb Threats

Bomb threats usually arrive by phone, though written and electronic threats occur too. How you handle the first moments of a threat call matters enormously for the response that follows.

If you receive a bomb threat by phone:

- Stay calm and let the caller finish speaking without interrupting.
- If your site has a bomb threat checklist near the phone, use it. If not, write down everything you can remember as soon as the call ends.
- Try to note: the exact wording of the threat, the caller's voice characteristics (masculine or feminine, accent, age estimate, calm or agitated), any background noise, and the exact time of the call.
- Ask questions if you can do so naturally: When will it go off? Where is it? What does it look like? Why are you doing this? Do not turn this into an interrogation, but gather what you can.
- Do not hang up first if the caller stays on the line. Let them end the call.
- Immediately after the call, notify your supervisor and call 911. Do not use two way radios or cell phones near the suspected threat area, since some devices can theoretically trigger certain explosive devices, though this risk is debated. Follow your site's specific policy on this.

General response to any bomb threat:

1. Notify police immediately. The decision to evacuate is typically made by police or by senior management based on the threat's credibility, not unilaterally by the guard on duty, unless your site's plan states otherwise.

2. If evacuation is ordered, follow the same evacuation procedures as a fire, but do not use elevators or activate the fire alarm unless directed, since alarm systems and elevators are sometimes considered potential trigger risks in specific threat scenarios.

3. Do not touch, move, or handle any suspicious object. Note its location and report it to police.

4. Assist police on arrival with any information you gathered.

Active Threat Situations

An active threat, meaning a person actively causing harm on your site, is the most severe scenario you may face. Canadian security and law enforcement generally teach the Run, Hide, Fight framework, adapted from similar international models.

- **Run:** If there is a safe path to escape the area, leave immediately. Leave belongings behind. Help others escape if you can do so without significant additional risk, but do not delay your own escape trying to convince others.

- **Hide:** If you cannot safely escape, find a place to hide that is out of the threat's view, and if possible, lock or barricade the door. Silence your phone and radio. Stay quiet.

- **Fight:** As an absolute last resort, if your life is in immediate danger and you cannot run or hide, use whatever is available to disrupt or disable the threat.

- **Call 911 as soon as it is safe to do so**, and provide the call taker with the location, number of people involved, and any description you have of the threat.

- **When police arrive**, follow their instructions immediately and exactly. Keep your hands visible. Do not point, yell, or run toward officers, since responding officers cannot immediately distinguish a guard from a threat in a chaotic scene.

Your role in an active threat is survival and information, not confrontation, except as an absolute last resort. Your training does not qualify you to engage an armed threat directly, and attempting to do so puts you and others at greater risk in most scenarios.

Medical Emergencies

Guards are often first on scene for a medical emergency, sometimes minutes before EMS can arrive.

1. Assess the scene for safety before approaching. Do not become a second casualty.
2. Call 911 immediately, or direct someone specifically to call while you begin care ("You, in the blue jacket, call 911 now").
3. Provide first aid within your training and certification level. Do not exceed your training.
4. If trained and equipment is available on site, use an AED for a suspected cardiac arrest as soon as possible.
5. Stay with the person until EMS arrives, and provide them with a clear handoff: what happened, what you observed, and what care you provided.
6. Control the scene, keeping bystanders back and maintaining the person's privacy and dignity as much as the situation allows.

Document the incident fully afterward, including timestamps for when you found the person, when you began care, and when EMS arrived.

Evacuation Procedures and Muster Points

Every building's fire safety plan designates specific evacuation routes and a muster point, a safe assembly location outside the building where evacuees gather.

- Know your site's evacuation routes for every area you patrol, not just your primary post.

- Know the muster point location and help direct evacuees there during an evacuation.
- Conduct or assist with a headcount at the muster point where your site's plan requires it, particularly for buildings with a defined occupant list, such as offices with sign in logs.
- Keep the muster point area clear of vehicle traffic and clear the path for arriving emergency vehicles.
- Report to arriving fire or police personnel with any information about missing individuals or people who may still be inside.

Severe Weather Response

Severe weather events, including tornadoes, extreme cold, flooding, and major winter storms, require specific responses depending on your region and site.

- Know your site's severe weather plan and shelter locations before a warning is issued.
- For tornado warnings, direct people to interior, windowless areas on the lowest floor available, away from glass.
- For extreme cold warnings, be alert for anyone outside your site who may need shelter, and know your site's policy on allowing access during an extreme weather emergency.
- For flooding, know which areas of your site are at risk and be prepared to restrict access to those areas.
- Monitor weather alerts through Environment Canada or your site's monitoring system, and pass along updates to your team and to building occupants as your site's plan directs.

The Core Principle Across Every Emergency

In every scenario in this section, the same sequence applies: assess safety, call for the right help immediately, follow your training and your site's specific plan, and document everything afterward. Do not improvise beyond your training, and do not hesitate to call 911 because you are unsure whether a situation is "serious enough." It is always better to make the call and stand down than to wait too long.

Remember:

- ★ You do not command.
- ★ You support.
- ★ They are the experts.
- ★ Safety first.

SECTION 10

HOW TO ASSIST LOCAL POLICE, FIRE, AND EMS

First responders need information, access, and cooperation.

Be calm.
Be clear.
Be helpful.
Be in their way.

POLICE

- Access
- Keys / Codes
- Location
- Hazards
- Witnesses
- Information
- Evidence

Preserve the scene.
Do not interfere.

FIRE

- Access
- Building info
- Utilities / Shut-offs
- Hazards (fire, gas, chemicals)
- Keys / Plans
- Evacuation status

Provide building information quickly.

EMS

- Access
- Location of patient
- Hazards
- Entry points
- Animals on site
- Any medical info you have

Direct them to the patient.

Meet responders here.

GIVE CLEAR INFORMATION

- ✓ What happened?
- ✓ Where is it?
- ✓ Who is involved?
- ✓ What hazards exist?
- ✓ What has been done?

BE READY TO PROVIDE

- ☐ Building access
- ☐ Keys / Gate codes
- ☐ Floor plans (if available)
- ☐ Contact information
- ☐ Incident details ★

YOU SUPPORT — THEY COMMAND.

★ Good teamwork = Better outcomes.

Section 10: How to Assist Local Police, Fire, and EMS

Your job during a real incident is not to replace first responders. It is to give them everything they need the moment they arrive, so they can do their job faster and more safely. This section covers what police, fire, and EMS actually expect from a security guard on scene.

What First Responders Expect From Security on Scene

First responders arriving at your site are working with almost no information until you give it to them. A guard who has already gathered and organized key facts saves precious time.

In general, responders expect you to:

- Have already called for the correct service and confirmed the call went through.
- Know the exact location of the incident within the building or property, not just the general address.
- Have basic facts ready: what happened, who is involved, and any immediate hazards.
- Stay out of their way once they arrive, unless they specifically ask for your help.
- Follow their instructions without debate, even if it differs from what you expected.

Responders do not expect you to have solved the problem before they arrive. They expect clear information and a clear path to the scene.

Handing Off a Scene Properly

A clean handoff is one of the most valuable things you can provide. Structure it the same way every time so you do not forget details under pressure.

Use this order when responders arrive:

1. **Identify yourself.** State your name and role clearly: "I'm the security guard on duty, I called this in."
2. **State what happened.** Give a short, factual summary, not a long narrative. Save detail for their questions.
3. **State the current situation.** Is the person still there? Still injured? Still a threat? Responders need to know what they are walking into right now, not just what happened five minutes ago.
4. **State what you have done.** Mention any first aid provided, any area you secured, or any people you moved or kept back.
5. **Point out hazards.** Any weapons, spills, blocked exits, or other dangers you are aware of.
6. **Offer to guide them.** Ask if they want you to lead them to the scene or stay back and let them proceed.

Keep this handoff under a minute where possible. Responders will ask follow up questions if they need more.

Providing Statements and Evidence

Once the immediate scene is stable, police may ask you for a formal statement. Treat this with the same care you use in your written reports.

- Stick to what you personally observed. If you are relaying something a witness told you, say so clearly: "A witness told me..." rather than presenting it as your own observation.
- Answer the question asked. Do not volunteer speculation or opinions about guilt, intent, or what "probably" happened.
- If you are unsure about a detail, say so directly. Guessing to sound more helpful damages your credibility and can complicate the investigation.
- Provide your written incident report to police if requested, and keep a copy for your employer's records.

- If you captured photos, video, or camera footage, let the officer know what exists and where it is stored. Do not delete, edit, or forward footage without direction from your employer or a documented lawful request from police.

Your statement may be used in an investigation or in court. Treat it with the same accuracy and restraint you use in your written reports.

Chain of Custody Basics

If you are asked to preserve evidence, whether it is an object, a piece of clothing, or digital footage, chain of custody matters. This means keeping a clear, unbroken record of who had control of the evidence and when.

- Do not handle a physical item more than necessary. Fingerprints, DNA, and other trace evidence degrade with handling.
- If you must move an item for safety reasons, note exactly what you moved, from where, to where, and at what time.
- Store any preserved item securely and note who has access to it until police take custody.
- For camera footage, note the exact time range relevant to the incident and flag it for retention immediately. Many systems overwrite footage automatically after a set period, so acting fast matters.
- Document every handoff: who you gave the evidence to, their name and badge number if it is an officer, and the exact time.

A broken chain of custody can make otherwise solid evidence unusable in court. When in doubt, touch less and document more.

Building Working Relationships With Local Police

Guards who have a working relationship with their local police get faster response times and better cooperation during incidents. This relationship is built over time, not created in the moment of an emergency.

- Introduce yourself to officers who patrol or respond to your area regularly, when the opportunity arises during a quiet moment.
- Share relevant site information proactively, such as known trespassing issues or recurring problem individuals, through the correct channel your employer allows.
- Follow up professionally after an incident if appropriate, without being a nuisance to a busy department.
- Respect officer time. Keep interactions focused and useful, not chatty, during active calls.

A guard known to local police as reliable, calm, and accurate gets taken seriously immediately. A guard known for exaggerated or unreliable reports gets deprioritized, even during a real emergency.

When to Call 911 vs Non-Emergency Lines

Knowing which line to call, and calling the right one quickly, matters as much as knowing what to say once connected.

Call 911 for:

- Any situation involving immediate danger to life or safety.
- Fire, active medical emergencies, or a crime in progress.
- Any situation where you are unsure how serious it is. When in doubt, 911 can redirect you if it turns out to be non-urgent, but a delayed 911 call for a genuine emergency cannot be undone.

Call the non-emergency line for:

- Reporting a completed crime with no immediate danger, such as discovering a break in after the fact with the suspect long gone.
- Requesting a police report for insurance purposes.
- General questions or non-urgent concerns about site security.

Keep your local non-emergency police number saved and posted at your site alongside emergency numbers. In a stressful moment, you do not want to be searching for a phone number you should already have on hand.

The Underlying Principle

Every part of this section comes down to the same goal: make the first responder's job easier the moment they step onto your site. Clear information, a clean handoff, careful evidence handling, and a track record of reliability all serve that single purpose. Responders remember guards who make their job easier, and that reputation follows you through your career.

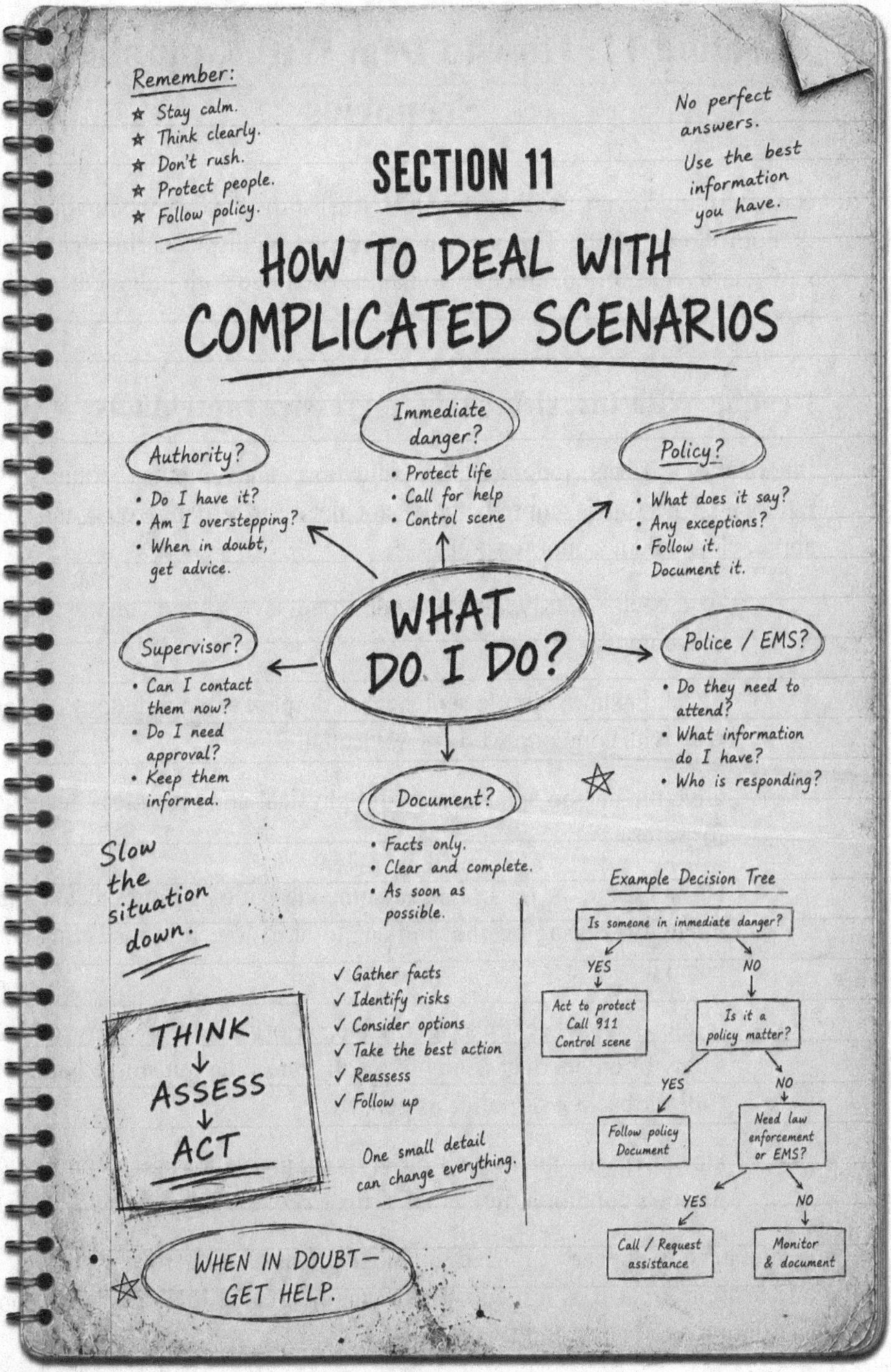
Remember:
Stay calm.
Think clearly.
Don't rush.
Protect people.
Follow policy.
SECTION 11
No perfect answers.
Use the best information you have.
HOW TO DEAL WITH COMPLICATED SCENARIOS
Immediate danger?
• Protect life
• Call for help
• Control scene
Authority?
• Do I have it?
• Am I overstepping?
• When in doubt, get advice.
Policy?
• What does it say?
• Any exceptions?
• Follow it.
Document it.
WHAT DO I DO?
Supervisor?
• Can I contact them now?
• Do I need approval?
• Keep them informed.
Police / EMS?
• Do they need to attend?
• What information do I have?
• Who is responding?
Document?
• Facts only.
• Clear and complete.
• As soon as possible.
Slow the situation down.
Example Decision Tree
Is someone in immediate danger?
YES
NO
Act to protect
Call 911
Control scene
Is it a policy matter?
YES
NO
Follow policy
Document
Need law enforcement or EMS?
YES
NO
Call / Request assistance
Monitor & document
✓ Gather facts
✓ Identify risks
✓ Consider options
✓ Take the best action
✓ Reassess
✓ Follow up
THINK
ASSESS
ACT
One small detail can change everything.
WHEN IN DOUBT—GET HELP.

Section 11: How to Deal With Complicated Scenarios

Basic training covers the fundamentals. Real shifts throw you situations that do not follow a script. This section walks through the scenarios that trip up new guards most often, and how to handle each one with judgment, not just procedure.

Dealing With Intoxicated or Aggressive Individuals

Intoxication affects judgment, coordination, and impulse control. An intoxicated person is unpredictable, not necessarily dangerous, and your approach should account for both.

- Approach calmly, keep your tone even, and avoid sudden movements.
- Speak in short, simple sentences. Complex reasoning does not land well with someone who is intoxicated.
- Give the person space and avoid physical contact unless necessary for safety.
- Do not argue or try to reason someone out of an intoxicated state. Focus on managing the immediate situation, not correcting their behavior.
- If the person becomes aggressive, prioritize your safety and the safety of others over trying to resolve the situation single handedly. Call for backup or police as needed.
- Document the interaction fully, including your observations of the person's condition, in factual terms as covered in Section 7.

If the person appears to need medical attention due to their level of intoxication, treat it as a medical situation and call EMS rather than only handling it as a behavioral issue.

Domestic Disputes on Property

Domestic disputes are among the most volatile situations you can encounter, precisely because the emotional history between the people involved is not visible to you.

- Do not attempt to mediate or resolve the dispute yourself. This is not your role, and inserting yourself into the middle of a domestic conflict increases risk to you.
- Keep a safe distance and monitor the situation without escalating it through your presence.
- Call police immediately if the dispute involves any physical altercation, threats, or if you believe someone is in danger.
- If asked to intervene by one party, remain neutral. Do not take sides or make judgments about who is at fault based on what you observe in a brief window.
- Prioritize separating the parties if it is safe to do so and both parties are willing, but do not physically force separation unless someone's immediate safety requires it.
- Document what you observed factually, without speculating about the relationship or history between the individuals.

Domestic situations on your property, particularly in residential buildings, may be recurring. Report patterns to your supervisor so property management can involve appropriate support resources if needed.

Trespassing and Unwanted Persons

Trespassing calls are routine, but handling them correctly protects you from liability.

- Confirm you have the authority to ask someone to leave. In most cases, this authority comes from your employer or the property owner, and it should be exercised consistently with your site's policy.

- State clearly and once that the person is trespassing and must leave the property.
- If the person refuses, do not escalate to physical removal on your own judgment alone. Understand your province's trespass legislation and your citizen's arrest limits, covered in Section 13, before you act.
- Call police if the person refuses to leave after a clear request, particularly if there is any history of conflict with this individual on your property.
- For repeat trespassers, check whether your site maintains a formal trespass notice or ban list, and follow the documented process rather than relying on memory of past incidents.

Avoid assuming someone is trespassing based on appearance alone. Confirm through your site's access procedures, such as checking a visitor log or asking who they are visiting, before making a judgment.

Suspected Criminal Activity

When you suspect a crime is occurring or about to occur, your role is to observe, document, and report, not to investigate or confront unless safety requires immediate action.

- Observe from a safe distance without alerting the individual that they are being watched, if possible.
- Note details as covered in Section 7: descriptions, times, plate numbers, and specific behavior observed.
- Contact police promptly, especially for anything involving weapons, theft in progress, or activity that suggests immediate danger.
- Do not attempt to detain someone unless you have clear legal grounds under your province's citizen's arrest provisions, and even then, only when it is safe to do so.

- Preserve any relevant camera footage immediately, since this evidence is often time limited before automatic overwrite.

Your value in these situations is often the quality of your observation and report, not direct intervention.

Mental Health Crises

Guards increasingly encounter individuals experiencing a mental health crisis, including psychiatric emergencies, severe anxiety, or dissociative episodes. These situations require patience and a different approach than a typical behavioral issue.

- Speak calmly and clearly, using simple language and short sentences.
- Give the person physical space. Crowding someone in crisis often increases distress.
- Avoid sudden movements, raised voices, or a large show of force unless the person poses an immediate danger to themselves or others.
- Do not argue with or attempt to correct what the person is experiencing, even if it does not reflect reality. Focus on safety, not correction.
- If the person is in danger of harming themselves or others, call 911 and specifically mention that this is a mental health crisis so responders can dispatch appropriately, including a mental health crisis team where available in your area.
- If you have completed mental health first aid training, apply it here. This training is one of the most valuable certifications for modern security work, as covered in Section 3.

Treat the person with the same dignity and patience you would want for a family member in crisis. Your calm presence can genuinely help de-escalate the situation.

Homeless Individuals on Private Property

This is one of the more delicate situations guards face regularly, particularly in urban postings. Balancing your duty to enforce property rules with basic human dignity requires judgment.

- Follow your site's specific policy on this issue. Many properties have clear guidelines on how to handle individuals sleeping or sheltering on the property.
- Approach with respect, not assumption. Not every unhoused person on your property is a problem, and treating everyone the same way regardless of behavior avoids unnecessary conflict.
- If asking someone to move along, do so calmly and clearly with respect, and be aware of extreme weather conditions that may make this a serious safety issue, not just a property issue.
- Know what local resources exist, such as shelters or outreach services, if your site or municipality provides this information to guards. Some cities have outreach teams you can contact instead of police for this specific situation.
- Escalate to police only when necessary, such as if the individual is engaging in disruptive or unsafe behavior beyond simply being present.

This is an area where your professionalism and judgment matter more than a rigid rule. Handle it with the same care you would want shown to anyone in a difficult circumstance. Treating someone with respect can go a long way to ending a situation favorably.

De-escalating Without Physical Contact

Across nearly every scenario in this section, the goal is the same: resolve the situation without physical contact whenever possible. Review Section 8's de-escalation basics, and apply them consistently:

- Lower your voice and slow your speech.

- Maintain a safe, non-threatening distance and body position.
- Give the person options rather than ultimatums where possible.
- Involve backup or police before a situation reaches a point where physical intervention feels like the only option.

Physical intervention should be your last resort, applied only when necessary for safety and always within the bounds of your training and your province's use of force law, covered in Section 13.

When and How to Use Force Legally

Sections 25 and 27 of the Canadian Criminal Code govern the use of force by any person, including security guards, in specific circumstances such as preventing a crime or making a lawful arrest. The law permits only the force that is reasonably necessary in the circumstances, not force in general.

Key principles to remember:

- Force must be proportional to the threat you are responding to.
- You cannot use force that is excessive relative to the situation, even if the other person acted first.
- Your authority to use force in a citizen's arrest is narrower than a police officer's authority. Understand these limits precisely, covered in full in Section 13.
- If you are trained and authorized to carry equipment like handcuffs or a baton, using that equipment outside your training or your employer's authorization exposes you to both criminal and civil liability.

When force becomes necessary, use the minimum required to control the situation safely, disengage as soon as it is safe to do so, and document the incident thoroughly and immediately afterward, following the format covered in Section 7.

The Judgment Behind Every Scenario

No handbook can script every situation you will face. What every scenario in this section shares is a consistent approach: assess safety first, de-escalate before you escalate, involve backup and police when a situation exceeds your role, and document everything with the same care regardless of how the incident is resolved. Build these habits, and you will handle the situations this section cannot predict just as well as the ones it can.

Remember:

- ★ Be professional.
- ★ Be consistent.
- ★ Be respectful.
- ★ Be accountable.

SECTION 12

CONDUCTING YOURSELF IN A PROFESSIONAL MANNER

YOU REPRESENT:

- ☐ Yourself
- ☐ Your employer
- ☐ Your client
- ☐ The profession

- Uniform.
- Language.
- Body language.
- Confidentiality.
- Integrity.

Someone is always watching.

★

Your choices reflect on everyone.

Section 12: Conducting Yourself in a Professional Manner

Your license gets you the job. Your conduct decides whether you keep it, get promoted, or get let go. Clients and employers judge guards constantly, often in small moments that never become an incident report. This section covers the standards that build a reputation you can build a career on.

Appearance and Uniform Standards

Your appearance is the first thing anyone on site notices, before you say a single word. It shapes whether people take your instructions seriously.

- Wear your uniform exactly as your employer specifies, including correct patches, badges, and any required equipment worn visibly.
- Keep your uniform clean and pressed. A wrinkled or stained uniform undermines your authority regardless of how competent you actually are.
- Follow grooming standards set by your employer, including hair, facial hair, and visible tattoo policies where they apply.
- Maintain proper footwear and equipment. Scuffed boots, running shoes, old distressed duty belt, and a dead flashlight all signal the same thing to a client… this guard is not on top of the details.
- Present yourself the same way on a slow Tuesday as you would if your regional manager walked through the door. Consistency is the standard, not an occasional effort.

Uniform standards exist because your appearance represents your employer's brand and the property you protect. Treat it accordingly, even when no one seems to be watching.

Communication Tone With the Public

How you speak matters as much as what you say. The public, tenants, and clients form an opinion of your entire company based on their interaction with you.

- Use a calm, respectful tone regardless of how the other person speaks to you. Matching an angry tone escalates the situation and reflects poorly on you.
- Address people politely, using "sir," "ma'am," or their name if known, unless your site's culture calls for something more casual.
- Keep instructions clear and direct without sounding harsh. "I need you to step back, please" lands better than a shouted "back off, now".
- Avoid slang, profanity, or overly casual language while on duty, even in a friendly exchange. Professional tone should be your default, not something you switch on only during a formal interaction.
- Listen fully before responding. Interrupting someone, even to correct them, damages the interaction and often makes de-escalation harder.

Every conversation you have on site is a small test of your professionalism. Treat routine interactions with the same care as high stakes ones, since the routine ones happen far more often and shape your overall reputation.

Confidentiality and Privacy Law

Security guards regularly access sensitive information: visitor logs, camera footage, incident details, and sometimes personal information about tenants or employees. Handling this correctly is both an ethical and a legal obligation.

Canada's federal privacy law, the Personal Information Protection and Electronic Documents Act (PIPEDA), governs how private sector organizations collect, use, and disclose personal information. As a guard, you interact with this law directly, even if you never read the act itself.

Practical rules to follow:

- Do not share information about incidents, tenants, or visitors with anyone outside your employer's approved reporting channels.
- Never post about your work, incidents, or people you encounter on social media, even without using names. Details can identify people even when names are removed.
- Handle camera footage strictly according to your employer's policy. Do not copy, forward, or share footage informally, even to "help" someone outside the proper process.
- If someone outside your organization, including a journalist, requests information about an incident, direct them to your supervisor or your employer's official contact. This is not your call to make individually.
- Store any written notes, logs, or reports securely, and follow your employer's retention and disposal policy rather than keeping personal copies.

Provinces including Quebec, British Columbia, and Alberta also have their own private sector privacy legislation that may apply alongside PIPEDA. Confirm with your employer which specific rules govern your site.

Avoiding Liability Through Professionalism

A large share of the legal risk in this industry comes not from major incidents, but from guards acting outside their authority or documenting things poorly. Professional conduct is your best protection.

- Stay within your trained role. Do not attempt tasks, like operating equipment or making legal judgment calls, that fall outside your training or license class.
- Follow your employer's policies exactly, even when you personally think a different approach would work better. Deviating from

policy, even with good intentions, creates liability if something goes wrong.

- Document consistently, as covered in Section 7. Inconsistent or incomplete documentation is one of the most common sources of liability exposure for guards and their employers.
- Know the limits of your authority precisely, particularly around use of force and citizen's arrest, covered in Sections 11 and 13.
- When uncertain about whether an action is within your authority, default to the more conservative choice and involve a supervisor or police rather than acting alone.

Professionalism is not just about manners. It is a practical, daily practice that protects you, your employer, and the people you interact with.

Ethics on the Job

Guards routinely have access to areas, information, and situations most people do not. That access comes with real ethical responsibility.

- Do not use your position for personal advantage, such as favors, discounts, or special treatment from tenants or clients.
- Report conflicts of interest to your supervisor, such as being asked to monitor or make decisions involving someone you know personally.
- Treat every person on your site with equal professionalism, regardless of their status, appearance, or how they treat you.
- Refuse gifts or gratuities that could be seen as compromising your objectivity, following your employer's specific policy on this.
- Report wrongdoing you observe, whether it involves a coworker, a tenant, or anyone else, through the correct channel, even when it feels uncomfortable to do so.

Your integrity, more than any single skill, determines whether people trust you with the responsibility this job carries.

Dealing With Client Complaints

Complaints happen in every service industry, and security is no exception. How you handle them shapes whether a complaint becomes a minor note or a serious problem for your career.

- Listen fully without becoming defensive, even if you believe the complaint is unfair.
- Acknowledge the person's concern directly: "I understand why that was frustrating" costs you nothing and de-escalates most situations.
- Avoid arguing your case in the moment. If you need to explain your actions, do so calmly and factually, without getting drawn into a back and forth.
- Report the complaint to your supervisor promptly and accurately, including your own account of what happened, rather than waiting to see if it goes away.
- Use legitimate complaints as a chance to improve. Not every complaint is baseless, and treating each one as a learning opportunity builds a stronger reputation over time than defensiveness ever will.

A guard who handles complaints with composure and accountability can earn more trust from employers and clients than a guard who never receives a complaint at all, because it shows you can handle friction professionally when it happens.

The Standard to Hold Yourself To

Professionalism in this job is not a performance for supervisors or clients watching closely. It is the standard you hold on the quiet shifts when no one is checking, because that consistency is exactly what earns trust, promotions, and a long career in this field.

Remember:

- ☆ Know the law.
- ☆ Know your limits.
- ☆ Stay in your lane.
- ☆ When in doubt, ask for guidance.

SECTION 13

LEGAL KNOWLEDGE EVERY GUARD NEEDS

You don't need to be a lawyer. You just need to understand enough to do your job the right way.

(!) Laws change. Your responsibility doesn't.

You are not here to enforce the law.

You are here to observe, report, and protect.

KEY AREAS

- Authority
- Consent
- Trespass
- Arrest
- Search
- Use of Force
- Privacy

KNOW THE LIMITS OF YOUR AUTHORITY.

This knowledge keeps you effective, professional, and out of trouble.

KNOW THE LAW.
RESPECT THE LAW.
STAY ON THE RIGHT SIDE OF IT.

Section 13: Legal Knowledge Every Guard Needs

You do not need a law degree to do this job well, but you do need a solid working understanding of the laws that define your authority. Guards who misunderstand their legal limits create liability for themselves and their employer. This section covers the core legal knowledge every Canadian security guard needs.

This section is a general overview, not legal advice. Laws and their interpretation change, and provincial variations exist. Consult your employer's legal counsel or a lawyer for guidance on a specific situation.

Citizen's Arrest Powers and Limits

Security guards are **not** peace officers. You **do not** have police powers. Your authority to arrest someone comes from the same section of the Criminal Code that applies to any private citizen: section 494.

Section 494(1) allows any person, including a guard, to arrest without a warrant:

- Someone found committing an indictable offence, or
- Someone who, on reasonable grounds, is believed to have committed a criminal offence and is being freshly pursued by people with lawful authority to arrest them.

Section 494(2) applies specifically to a property owner, someone in lawful possession of property, or a person authorized by the owner, which typically includes a security guard working that property. This subsection allows an arrest without a warrant of a person found committing a criminal offence on or in relation to that property. Following amendments made through the Citizen's Arrest and Self-defence Act, this arrest can also happen within a reasonable time after the offence, if you believe on reasonable grounds that it is not feasible for a police officer to make the arrest instead.

Section 494(3) requires that anyone arrested under this section be delivered to a peace officer immediately. You cannot hold someone indefinitely. Your role is to detain briefly and hand off to police, not to conduct an extended detention or investigation.

Section 494(4) connects this arrest power to section 25 of the Criminal Code, which protects a person acting under proper legal authority, including reasonable force used during a lawful arrest.

Key limits to remember:

- Your arrest authority applies to criminal offences, meaning federal offences under the Criminal Code or other federal legislation. It does not extend to provincial or municipal violations, such as a bylaw infraction.
- The distinction between indictable and summary conviction offences matters. Your grounds for arrest are more limited with summary offences, which are the less serious category.
- Any force used during an arrest must be reasonable and proportional to the circumstances. Excessive force during an otherwise lawful arrest can itself become a criminal or civil liability.
- After an arrest, hand the person to police as soon as possible. Do not attempt to interrogate, search beyond immediate safety needs, or hold the person longer than necessary.

A wrongful arrest, even one made in good faith, can expose you and your employer to civil liability for false imprisonment. When in doubt about whether grounds for arrest exist, observe, document, and call police instead of acting.

Trespass to Property Acts by Province

Every province has its own trespass legislation governing who can be told to leave a property and what happens if they refuse. These acts typically work alongside, not instead of, your Criminal Code arrest powers.

General principles across most provincial trespass acts:

- The owner, occupier, or an authorized agent, which includes a security guard acting for the property, can direct a person to leave.
- Failing to leave after being directed to do so is itself an offence under the applicable provincial act, separate from any Criminal Code offence.
- Provincial trespass acts generally allow arrest without warrant for a trespass offence in progress, in addition to the Criminal Code powers already covered, though the specific conditions vary by province.
- Penalties for trespass violations are typically fines under provincial law, not criminal convictions, unless the conduct also violates the Criminal Code.

Because trespass law is provincial, the exact name of the act, the specific wording, and the penalties differ by jurisdiction: Ontario's Trespass to Property Act, British Columbia's Trespass Act, Alberta's Petty Trespass Act and Trespass to Premises Act, and equivalent legislation in other provinces. Learn the specific act that applies in your province, and confirm your employer has provided training on how it applies to your specific site.

Use of Force Law

Sections 25 through 27 of the Criminal Code govern the use of force by any person, including security guards.

- **Section 25** protects a person who is required or authorized by law to do something in the administration or enforcement of the law, provided they act on reasonable grounds and use no more force than necessary.
- **Section 27** allows the use of reasonable force to prevent the commission of an offence that would likely cause immediate and serious injury to a person or property.

The core principle across this entire area of law is proportionality. Force must match the level of threat you are actually facing, not the level of threat you feared might develop. Using more force than necessary, even against someone who was initially in the wrong, can expose you to assault charges or civil liability.

Review Section 11 of this handbook for practical scenario guidance, and Section 3 for training requirements tied to any equipment you may be authorized to carry.

Privacy Law Basics

Security work involves constant contact with personal information: names, images, movements, and sometimes sensitive personal circumstances. Canada's federal Personal Information Protection and Electronic Documents Act (PIPEDA) governs how private sector organizations, including most security employers, handle this information. Several provinces, including Quebec, British Columbia, and Alberta, have their own private sector privacy legislation that may apply instead of or alongside PIPEDA.

Practical implications for you as a guard:

- Camera footage and incident records are personal information subject to privacy law. Handle and share them strictly according to your employer's policy.
- You do not have unrestricted authority to record, photograph, or share information about individuals beyond what your role and your employer's policy require.
- Requests for information from outside your organization, including police requests outside a clear legal process, should go through your supervisor, not be handled independently by you on shift.

Review Section 12 for the practical conduct rules that flow from these legal obligations.

Liability and When Guards Can Be Sued

Guards and their employers can face civil liability in several common scenarios:

- **False imprisonment**, resulting from an arrest made without proper legal grounds.
- **Assault or battery**, resulting from force that exceeds what was reasonable and necessary.
- **Negligence**, resulting from a failure to act reasonably, such as ignoring a known hazard or failing to respond appropriately to a foreseeable risk.
- **Defamation**, resulting from false statements made about an individual, including in a written report or a verbal accusation that turns out to be unfounded.
- **Privacy violations**, resulting from improper handling or disclosure of personal information, including camera footage.

The best protection against liability is consistent, well documented, policy compliant conduct. Guards who act within their training, follow employer policy, and document thoroughly are far better protected than guards who improvise, even when the improvisation comes from good intentions.

Testifying in Court

Some incidents you handle may eventually lead to a court appearance, whether as a witness for the Crown, in a civil suit, or in a regulatory hearing. Preparation matters.

- Review your written report thoroughly before testifying. Your report is often the only record of your memory from months or years earlier, and inconsistencies between your report and your testimony damage your credibility.
- Answer only the question asked. Do not volunteer additional information, speculation, or opinion unless specifically asked.
- Stick to what you personally observed. If asked about something you did not witness directly, say so clearly rather than guessing.

- Stay calm under cross examination. A lawyer's job in cross examination is often to find inconsistencies or provoke a reaction. Answer steadily regardless of tone or pressure.
- Dress and present yourself professionally, consistent with the standards covered in Section 12.
- If you do not understand a question, ask for clarification rather than guessing at what is being asked.

Guards who write clear, factual reports at the time of an incident make testifying far easier months or years later. This is one more reason the report writing habits in Section 7 matter beyond the immediate aftermath of an incident.

The Foundation This Section Provides

Every legal principle in this section points toward the same practical rule: know your authority precisely, stay within it, and document everything. When you are unsure whether an action falls within your legal authority, the safer choice is almost always to observe, document, and call police rather than to act unilaterally. This approach protects the people you interact with, your employer, and your own career.

Remember:

- ☆ Keep learning.
- ☆ Stay humble.
- ☆ Help others.
- ☆ Build your reputation.
- ☆ Opportunities come to prepared people.

SECTION 14

CAREER GROWTH

This career can take you further than you think.

SECURITY GUARD
↓
SENIOR GUARD
↓
SUPERVISOR
↓
SITE MANAGER
↓
OPERATIONS / MANAGEMENT

SPECIALIST PATHS

- INVESTIGATIONS
- TRAINING
- RISK MANAGEMENT
- LOSS PREVENTION
- EXECUTIVE PROTECTION
- EMERGENCY MANAGEMENT
- COMPLIANCE / AUDIT
- CONSULTING
- CORPORATE SECURITY

Your attitude and effort determine your ceiling.

EXPERIENCE + TRAINING + REPUTATION
=
OPPORTUNITY ☆

Never stop improving.

What's next?

KEYS TO MOVING FORWARD:

- ✓ Stay reliable.
- ✓ Take initiative.
- ✓ Solve problems.
- ✓ Communicate well.
- ✓ Get the right training.
- ✓ Be a leader.
- ✓ Treat people right.
- ✓ Protect your reputation.

Notes:

Section 14: Career Growth

Most guards start this job to pay the bills or to test the waters of a career they are curious about. What happens next is up to you. This industry offers real paths upward, and the guards who advance are almost always the ones who treated their entry level role as a foundation, not a ceiling.

Moving Into Supervision or Management

Supervisor and manager roles are the most common next step for guards who want to stay in the industry and grow their income and responsibility.

What employers look for when promoting from within:

- A consistent track record of reliability: showing up on time, completing reports correctly, and following procedure without repeated correction.
- Demonstrated judgment during real incidents, reflected in clear reports and sound decisions under pressure.
- Willingness to take on additional responsibility, such as training new hires or covering extra shifts when needed.
- Basic leadership skills: clear communication, fairness, and the ability to hold coworkers accountable without creating conflict.

Practical steps to position yourself:

- Tell your current supervisor directly that you are interested in advancement. Many promotions go to guards who express interest, not just guards who happen to be noticed.
- Take on informal leadership opportunities when they arise, such as training a new guard or taking point during a team response.
- Pursue supervisor specific training if your employer offers it, covering scheduling, performance management, and client relations.

- Learn the business side of your site: client expectations, contract terms, and how your company measures site performance. Supervisors are expected to understand this, not just security procedures.

Transitioning to Policing or Corrections

Many guards use security work as a deliberate stepping stone toward a policing or corrections career. Recruiters at many Canadian police services and correctional agencies view relevant security experience favorably, since it demonstrates familiarity with report writing, use of force principles, dealing with the public, and working within a structured legal framework.

If this is your goal:

- Seek out postings that expose you to a wide range of incident types, since breadth of experience strengthens an application more than time in a single quiet posting.
- Build a strong, clean record. Any disciplinary issue or license infraction can affect a future policing or corrections application.
- Pursue physical fitness standards early. Most policing and corrections agencies have specific fitness testing requirements, and starting preparation years in advance makes a real difference.
- Research the specific application requirements and hiring process for the agencies you are targeting well before you plan to apply, since some processes take a year or longer from application to offer.
- Ask serving officers or correctional staff, if you have the opportunity, what security experience they found most valuable when they made the same transition.

Starting Your Own Security Company

Experienced guards with a strong understanding of licensing, contracts, and client relationships sometimes move into business ownership, either running their own guard company or working as an independent contractor in specialized fields like investigation or consulting.

Before pursuing this path, understand what it actually requires:

- A business license, in addition to your personal security license, and often a separate security business or agency license depending on your province's requirements.
- Commercial general liability insurance and, in most cases, bonding for your guards.
- A solid understanding of contract terms, client acquisition, and staffing, which are business skills separate from security skills.
- Enough industry experience and contacts to win your first contracts. Most successful security business owners spent years building a reputation and a network before starting their own company.

This path carries real financial risk and demands business skills beyond security expertise. Guards considering it benefit from working under an experienced business owner first, whether through direct employment or mentorship, before striking out independently.

Networking Within the Industry

Career growth in security, like most industries, depends heavily on who knows your work, not just what you know.

- Join a professional association relevant to your specialization. The Canadian Association of Security and Investigation Services (CANASA) and Canadian chapters of ASIS International both offer networking, training, and industry credibility for members serious about the field.
- Attend industry conferences, training sessions, and local chapter events where available. These are where supervisors, hiring managers, and business owners meet the people they later hire or promote.

- Stay in touch with former supervisors and coworkers as you move between employers. This industry is smaller than it looks, and a good reputation follows you between companies.
- Consider pursuing an industry recognized credential, such as a Certified Protection Professional (CPP) designation through ASIS International, if you are aiming for a senior security management role over the long term.

Building a Long Term Career, Not Just a Job

The guards who build the strongest careers in this industry share a few common habits, regardless of which specific path they pursue:

- They treat every posting, no matter how routine, as an opportunity to build a reputation for reliability and sound judgment.
- They invest in training beyond the minimum required for licensing, as covered in Section 3.
- They document consistently and communicate professionally, as covered in Sections 7 and 12, because these habits are what employers and clients actually remember.
- They stay curious about the parts of the industry they have not yet worked in, whether that means trying a new posting type, pursuing a new certification, or learning the business side of the work.

This career rewards patience and consistency more than any single dramatic moment. Show up, do the work well, and the opportunities in this section will find you faster than you expect.

Keep this section handy.
The right information at the right time.
Quick Reminders:
☆ Stay observant.
☆ Document everything.
☆ Follow policy.
☆ Ask if unsure.
☆ Stay professional.
REFERENCE
FORMS
CHECKLISTS
QUICK GUIDES
APPENDICES
Keep this section handy.
Important Numbers
• Police 911
• Fire 911
• Ambulance 911
• Non-Emergency
• Supervisor
• Site Office
Notes to Self:
✓ Read the handbook.
✓ Know the site.
✓ Learn the people.
✓ Stay calm.
✓ Do the right thing.
Main Entrance
Office
Parking
Rear Exit
"Preparation today prevents problems tomorrow."

Appendices

Appendix A: Provincial and Territorial Licensing Contacts

Contact details, fees, and requirements change over time. Confirm current information directly with each regulator before relying on it. Where a specific phone number or address is not listed below, use the department's general contact line or website to reach the correct office.

Ontario Private Security and Investigative Services Branch, Ministry of the Solicitor General Email: PrivateSecurity@ontario.ca Phone: 416-212-1650 (Toronto area), toll free 1-866-767-7454 Mail: ServiceOntario Occupational Licensing Services Office, PO Box 4500, Kingston, ON K7L 0E1

Alberta Security Programs, Alberta Justice Mail: PO Box 1023 Station Main, Edmonton, AB T5J 2M1 Phone: 1-877-462-0791

British Columbia Security Programs Division, Ministry of Public Safety and Solicitor General Training approval coordinated with the Justice Institute of British Columbia.

Quebec Bureau de la sécurité privée (BSP) Governs licensing under the Loi sur la sécurité privée.

Saskatchewan Private Investigators and Security Guards Program, Safer Communities Enforcement Services, Ministry of Justice and Attorney General Mail: 485 Maxwell Crescent, Regina, SK S4N 5X9 Phone: 306-787-5496 Email: pisg@gov.sk.ca Note: Saskatchewan licenses individuals through their employer. You cannot apply for a license without a licensed security business sponsoring you.

Manitoba Private Investigators and Security Guards Program, Manitoba Justice Governs licensing under The Private Investigators and Security Guards Act.

Nova Scotia Security Programs Office, Department of Justice, Policing and Victim Services Division Phone: 902-424-0859, toll free 1-888-760-5577 Governs licensing under the Security and Investigative Services Act.

New Brunswick Private Investigators and Security Services licensing, Service New Brunswick / Department of Justice and Public Safety Governs licensing under the Private Investigators and Security Services Act.

Prince Edward Island Security Programs Office, Department of Justice and Public Safety Governs licensing under the Private Investigators and Security Guards Act. Note: as of this writing, PEI does not mandate a specific training or testing course as a licensing condition. Confirm current requirements directly with the department, since this is one of the areas most likely to change.

Newfoundland and Labrador Consumer and Financial Services Division, Digital Government and Service NL Governs licensing under the province's private investigation, security guard, and burglar alarm regulations.

Yukon, Northwest Territories, and Nunavut None of the three territories currently maintain a dedicated, standalone security guard licensing regime comparable to the provinces. Requirements, where they exist, are typically addressed through general business licensing and federal or territorial employment standards rather than a specific security licensing branch. Contact your territorial department of justice or the equivalent business licensing office directly to confirm current requirements before working in any of the territories, since this is an area where rules can change with little public notice.

Appendix B: Sample Forms

Patrol Log Template

Site: ________________________ Date: _______________

Guard Name: _________________ License #: ___________

Shift Start: _______ Shift End: _______

Time | Location Checked | Observations

Time	Location Checked	Observations

Doors/Gates Secured: Y / N Notes: _______________

Lighting Issues: Y / N Notes: _______________

Fire Exits Clear: Y / N Notes: _______________

Guard Signature: ____________ Time Completed: ______

Incident Report Template

Site: ________________________ Date: _______________

Guard Name: _________________ License #: ___________

Time Incident Occurred: _______ Time Reported: _______

Exact Location: _____________________________________

Persons Involved (name/description):

____

Chronological Account:

____

____

____

Actions Taken:

____

Outcome:

____

Witnesses (name/contact if available):

____

Supervisor Notified: Y / N Name: _____ Time: _____

Police Notified: Y / N Report #: __________

Camera Footage Flagged: Y / N Time Range: ________

Guard Signature: _________ Report Completed: _____

Use of Force Report Template

Site: ___________________ Date: ____________

Guard Name: _____________ License #: ________

Time of Incident: ______ Exact Location: ________

Subject Description: __________________________

Reason Force Was Used: ________________________

Type of Force Used: ___________________________

Duration: ____________

Injuries to Subject: Y / N Description: __________

Injuries to Guard: Y / N Description: __________

Chronological Account:

____

____

Witnesses:

____

Supervisor Notified: Y / N Name: ______ Time: ______

Police Notified: Y / N Report #: ____________

Camera Footage Flagged: Y / N Time Range: __________

Guard Signature: ___________ Report Completed: ______

Appendix C: NATO Phonetic Alphabet Chart

Letter	Code Word
A	Alpha
B	Bravo
C	Charlie
D	Delta
E	Echo
F	Foxtrot
G	Golf
H	Hotel
I	India
J	Juliett
K	Kilo
L	Lima
M	Mike
N	November
O	Oscar
P	Papa
Q	Quebec
R	Romeo
S	Sierra
T	Tango
U	Uniform
V	Victor
W	Whiskey
X	X-ray
Y	Yankee
Z	Zulu

Appendix D: Emergency Contact Template

SITE EMERGENCY CONTACTS

Emergency (Police/Fire/EMS): 911

Non-Emergency Police: ____________________

Site Supervisor: __________________________

Regional Manager: _________________________

Building Maintenance: _____________________

Gas Utility Emergency Line: _______________

Electrical Utility Emergency Line: ________

Poison Control: 1-844-764-7669 (Canada, general line - confirm your provincial line)

Nearest Hospital: _________________________

Muster Point Location: ____________________

Appendix E: Glossary of Security Terms

AED - Automated External Defibrillator, used to treat sudden cardiac arrest.

Chain of custody - The documented, unbroken record of who has handled a piece of evidence and when.

Citizen's arrest - An arrest made by a private person, including a security guard, under section 494 of the Criminal Code, rather than by a peace officer.

CRJMC - Criminal Record and Judicial Matters Check, the background check standard used in Ontario licensing.

De-escalation - Techniques used to reduce the intensity of a conflict or crisis without physical intervention.

Indictable offence - A more serious category of criminal offence under the Criminal Code, generally carrying broader arrest powers than a summary offence.

Muster point - A designated safe assembly location outside a building where occupants gather during an evacuation.

PIPEDA - Personal Information Protection and Electronic Documents Act, Canada's federal private sector privacy law.

Plain language - Radio communication using everyday words instead of coded terminology, now the standard across most Canadian policing and increasingly private security.

PSISA - Private Security and Investigative Services Act, Ontario's governing legislation for the security industry.

Static post - A security posting where a guard remains at a single fixed location for the duration of a shift.

Summary conviction offence - A less serious category of criminal offence under the Criminal Code, generally carrying more limited arrest powers than an indictable offence.

Trespass to Property Act - Provincial legislation (name varies by province) governing the right to direct a person to leave, and the penalties for refusing.

WHMIS - Workplace Hazardous Materials Information System, mandatory training for handling hazardous materials in many worksites.

Appendix F: Further Reading and Resources

- Your provincial or territorial security licensing regulator's official website (see Appendix A) for current legislation, forms, and requirements.
- The Criminal Code of Canada, available through the Justice Laws Website (laws-lois.justice.gc.ca), for the full text of sections referenced throughout this handbook.
- Canadian Association of Security and Investigation Services (CANASA), for industry news, training, and networking.
- ASIS International, Canadian chapters, for advanced certifications including the Certified Protection Professional (CPP) designation.
- Your employer's specific site procedures and emergency plans, which take priority over the general guidance in this handbook for any conflict between the two.

This handbook gives you a strong foundation. Your specific employer, site, and province will add detail and requirements beyond what any general guide can cover. Treat this book as a starting point for your career, not the final word on any single topic.

www.ingramcontent.com/pod-product-compliance
Lightning Source LLC
LaVergne TN
LVHW041208061126
851857LV00018B/1985